Acclaim for Chigozie Enwereuzo's *Estate Planning 101*

A Beginner's Guide to Transferring Assets to Heirs in Nigeria

"A candid and comprehensive look at how to plan your estate for everyone—from students to practitioners. The author has demonstrated her mastery of estate planning from years of experience in teaching the subject at the Institute of Financial Planning (IFP)."

—Friday Orjieh
Managing Director/CEO
UNIC Insurance Plc.

"Chigozie' s style of writing makes the book very easy to read and understand. It presents WILL writing as a standard requirement or natural responsibility of everyone in tidying up one's affairs personally the way one desires. It thus sort of takes the myth and scare out of WILL writing.

The questions and teasers at the end of each chapter help the reader to reflect on what had been read. Besides, it offers very clear and distinct ways of distributing assets during and after one's life on planet earth.

I commend the book to everyone who is interested in distributing his/her assets to his/her loved ones in the preferred (manner) with the view of entrenching lasting peace so that one could indeed REST IN PEACE ETERNALLY."

—Helen Ideleli Jemerigbe (Mrs.)
Director
Technical Skill Development Project
Nigeria Employers' Consultative Association (NECA)

"Chigozie Enwereuzo ignited a flame of enthusiasm in me with her teachings on estate planning. The knowledge gained from the course, fully captured in her new book on the subject, has been very relevant to my job responsibilities. Thank you, this will have an everlasting value. May your honesty and advice return to you many times over and again."

—Okeremute Ben Iwhiwhu
Sales and Wealth Distribution
Stanbic IBTC Asset Management Limited

"I perceived Chigozie Enwereuzo's teaching (on estate planning) to be very informative and interactive. The discussions and practical examples contributed immensely to the knowledge I acquired during the estate planning course. Her teaching of the subject made a great impact on me. After attending the course, I decided to set up some insurance and educational scheme for myself and family."

—Moses Odeli
On-the-Job Learning Specialist
Chevron

"As a lawyer, writer, and teacher, Chigozie Enwereuzo is coming on the fast lane. Her work on estate planning proved to be more comprehensive than what I thought in that area of study. What I enjoyed most about the course is the teacher's thorough pedagogic voice, which ran throughout the breadth of the instructional text in the manner of a teacher earnestly committed to the art of human development, teaching, and learning. As a former student, I found Chigozie's instructional text to be very comprehensive and painstakingly researched, which she taught professionally. Her book—*Estate Planning 101*—is a compendium. . . . I recommend the book without hesitation to the general public . . . as a classic reference work for aspiring estate planners.

—Tonnie Ofulue
Civil Servant (Delta State)
Successful participant (Certificate in Financial Planning program)

"I once attended a financial training program, and Chigozie happened to be one of the facilitators. The methods (of estate planning) she taught were really impressive and relatable, leaving a lifelong mark. After four years, I still hear her words subtly guiding some of my decisions."

—Temitope Jemerigbe
Managing Director
DKK

"I already owned several books about estate planning when I went for a three months financial planning program—one of the major courses being Estate Planning, handled by the author. The books I had were pretty comprehensive, but they went into far more detail than I really needed, and I wound up not doing as much as I should have since I was more confused than anything trying to digest all the different kinds of information on trusts, etc. However, this book—*Estate Planning 101*—gets right to the heart of the various topics it covers (and is pretty funny in some places too!). It doesn't try to be an encyclopedia or a book for estate-planning lawyers. But it succeeds at what it does apparently intend to do, which is help the average person like me understand just what I need to concentrate on for my estate planning and what I don't need to worry about. The good news is that after reading this book, I now have a much better idea of what my estate planning needs to include. The bad news is that I also realize how much I still have to do! Fortunately, I have a pretty good road map now. I strongly recommend this book to anyone who wants to get a handle on everything that estate planning includes (which I didn't realize was nearly as much as the author's cover)."

—Adesanwo Morayo Adebowale
Head, Financial Control and Admin.
Dunbell Securities Limited

ESTATE PLANNING 101

A BEGINNER'S GUIDE TO TRANSFERRING ASSETS TO HEIRS IN NIGERIA

CHIGOZIE ENWEREUZO

LifeLongLearning Books

Printed in the United States of America.

Library of Congress Control Number: 2021949749

ISBN	Paperback	978-1-68536-129-7
	eBook	978-1-68536-130-3

Westwood Books Publishing LLC
Atlanta Financial Center
3343 Peachtree Rd NE Ste 145-725
Atlanta, GA 30326

www.westwoodbookspublishing.com

To my family—Daddy, Mummy, Halo, and Nna—for your love and support, and for keeping me grounded.

The most unfair thing about life is the way it ends . . .

—Source Unknown

CONTENTS

FOREWORD

Estate planning sets out your own plan for how your assets should be distributed in the event of your passing. This subject can be hard to deal with emotionally, and particularly in our society, it is largely a fear of dying that prevents many people from dwelling on estate matters. Yet by admitting your own mortality and dealing with your eventual demise by putting your affairs in order, you can bring much relief to yourself, ease the transition for loved ones, and soften the impact of your death on them. Careful planning can eliminate much of the feeding frenzy that can occur after a person dies.

Chigozie Enwereuzo's *Estate Planning 101* is comprehensive, up-to-date, and easy-to-read and addresses the common questions relating to estate planning. It also provides tips and strategies for the most appropriate estate plan and highlights the various estate-planning tools. Her discussions include practical, vivid examples that underscore the critical importance of an estate plan. She has also managed to infuse a touch of humor in the midst of what is regarded as morbid; this helps to allay some of the fears and much of the confusion associated with this sensitive subject. Its broad coverage will appeal to the novice as well as the seasoned professional.

I recommend this book to students, teachers, professionals, families, and all those interested in deepening their knowledge and maximizing their wealth through estate planning and who wish to take control of their personal financial life and legacy.

Chigozie's *Estate Planning 101* is one of those books you should keep within reach as a comprehensive resource for all your estate-planning concerns. She provides straightforward guidelines for a wide range of estate-planning scenarios. Tailored to the Nigerian setting but, at the same time, most relevant to a wide range of audiences, it is an invaluable resource and shall serve as a reference point for years to come on our bookshelves.

—Nimi Akinkugbe
Regional Director (West Africa)
Barclays

PREFACE

In late 2005, my boss, the late F. N. Akpe, called me to his office for a lengthy conversation that led to his giving me what I considered then to be an onerous task.

The conversation was about his long-nurtured but yet-to-be fulfilled vision of successfully promoting a new profession of personal financial planners and advisers in the country. The task was for me to take responsibility for making that vision a successful reality.

Part of that assignment included my teaching a course on estate planning. It was one of the courses taught at a pioneer certificate-awarding, professional foundation program on personal financial planning that the organization he headed ran in collaboration with the consultancy unit of the University of Lagos for some years. It was important for me to teach the subject from a Nigerian perspective.

It was while conducting the research I needed to develop content on the subject that reality hit me: there was not a single material at the time—books or articles—written specifically on the subject of estate planning for the Nigerian space. I literally had to start from ground zero.

Working on this book, I had to factor in the peculiar legal system operational in Nigeria. Customary laws, statutes, and the adopted common law from our colonial rulers all apply simultaneously in the country. I had to utilize available materials relevant to the country, guided by the core issues on which estate-planning activities are based globally, as well as information gathered from numerous interviews I conducted.

In recent years, awareness of the need for estate planning has risen sharply in Nigeria. Shocked by the stock market slide and the investment losses suffered by many and the fall from grace, as it were, of the banking sector and the victims that the fall took with it, many people in active life began new journeys of introspection. Their realization that nothing seemingly is certain anymore led to deep desires to plan for uncertainty and make plans for dependents, especially nuclear families.

The writing of *Estate Planning 101*, which has taken me over seven years to conclude, was helped by the quality feedback, questions, and one-on-one interactions I had with students of that program. My estate-planning advisory work also opened my eyes to some trending issues and practices that were previously considered unacceptable in our clime. Eureka moments that my small but very discerning crop of clients shared with me as well as the challenges they have had to grapple with along the way further gave me the energy to finish this book.

Arguably a pioneering work on the subject, *Estate Planning 101* presents a road map for the not-so-new skill of planning for estates in Nigeria, a straightforward and comprehensive information for discerning initiators keen to commence their own planning activities but wary of groping in the dark. Reading this book assures you that success in planning your estate will be maximized while minimizing mistakes.

The book is divided into four parts. Part 1 progressively addresses the need for estate planning and how it developed in Nigeria. Part 2 discusses the essential components of modern estate planning. Part 3 deals with the tools required to attain effective and successful end results after the planning. Part 4 discusses the importance of preparing in advance for elderly life and incapacity (should it occur) and, finally, planning for your body parts and intangible legacy.

The need for the information in this book has become crucial in our environment but, knowing our cultural beliefs and practices as it has to do with death and all matters related to it, it will take courage and an open mind to embrace the practice prescribed in it.

While I embarked on an extensive research work to put *Estate Planning 101* together, information given in it is for general knowledge and should not be wholly relied upon when making fundamental decisions when commencing the plan of your estate. The advice of a qualified legal practitioner versed in estate planning and related matters must be sought for best results.

ACKNOWLEDGMENT

I would like to thank my family for their tremendous show of love, care, and support during my research and long nights of writing *Estate Planning 101*. My finishing this work at this time would most probably have been unachievable without their care.

My gratitude goes to Carol Ekperikoro for helping with the typing of some of the materials I used and Tonnie Ofulue for his administrative support during my years of facilitating the subject at the University of Lagos Consultancy Unit.

The feedback, commentary, and evaluation I have received from hundreds of participants that have attended my estate-planning modules enriched my research strategy. Mrs. Helen Jemerigbe and Mrs. Nimi Akinkugbe were particularly helpful as they have kept in touch long after attending my class, offering me fantastic, dispassionate, and constructive criticisms that I have found very useful while writing this book.

I thank my dad, Cosmas Enwereuzo, for helping with the editing of the first draft before he had to discontinue for health reasons. My Mum has been my best fan and, as always, cheered me on during those tiring phases when I experienced serious doses of writer's block. Thank you, Nna, for letting me be whenever I needed those quiet times to push my writing.

they needed an estate plan. However, Aigbe replied, "Estate plan? We don't need an estate plan. All we might need is a simple will."

Was he right? What is an estate? What is an estate plan? Is it different from a will? What can an estate plan do for Aigbe and Esse? How can they go about accomplishing all the things they talked about? Can anything in an estate plan help them if they become incapacitated now or at old age?

Our Estate-Planning Reality

You are living and have acquired substantial (in your estimate) assets or wealth. Have you thought about what will happen to them when you die?

In Nigeria, we do not like talking about dying and death or anything remotely connected to that subject. It's almost a taboo subject for discussions. Indeed, anyone bringing up the subject of death without something leading to it is deemed to be bringing about a bad omen either to oneself or others or having sinister intentions!

The reality, however, is that if you do not take the necessary steps to plan for the management and disposition of that business, property, asset, or investment you have spent a lifetime building, it may be used, taken over, inherited, or distributed in a manner you never imagined possible!

You need to brace up and ask yourself the following questions:

- Have I made plans to preserve everything I own and worked for all my life?
- Who and how will they be treated, taken care of, or distributed when I go to meet my ancestors?
- What if the person that ends up taking over my property when I die is that same person I would never have allowed to go near anything I own?
- Will my wife and children automatically take over my property? Do I really want them to be able to do that?
- Who exactly do I want to inherit any part of what belongs to me after I am dead and gone?

Attempting to answer these questions will help you determine the current state of your entire assets or wealth and whether you need an estate plan.

Aigbe and Esse's challenges constitute some of the numerous life situations we deal with in our daily lives and which brings the importance of estate planning to the fore. The need to be aware of carefully thought-out estate plans and the benefits of using them to protect property and legacies while helping to prevent unhappiness and rancor among family and loved ones is now at an all-time high.

Know What Is Available

Before you can create a plan that will provide for your family and loved ones, you need to know what types of documents and legal arrangements are available to you. Some documents are easier to create while you are alive but are more expensive for your family and loved ones after you are gone. Other documents are more challenging to create now but will save your family and loved ones a substantial amount of money as well as unnecessary hassles.

There are five primary ways by which property can pass: a will, a trust, joint property, and certain types of contracts if you choose to use them to pass them to your chosen family members and others or through intestacy or if you choose not to prepare any document for that purpose—in which case the government chooses to distribute your property on your behalf, as it prefers. Each of these methods of planning comes with advantages and disadvantages.

Leaving a Legacy

A well-designed plan can make your dreams live on even after your death. If you do not have a plan, your family might never know what your dream was. Even if your dream was known, it may not be realized because a huge chunk of your money and property is being spent on legal fees and taxes that could have been saved if you had understood the rules and had a plan in place.

Wills, trusts, probates, annuities, and retirement plans are all tools you can use to leave your own legacy—for your family, friends, and possibly, your community. You will learn what tools you have to work with and how to use them to their maximum effect. While some of these tools are designed to help after you are gone, some of them will help you accumulate or retain more of your wealth while you are living. Learn the rules and let your dreams live on!

Becoming familiar with the rules of estate planning and what strategies are available to you during the preplanning stages will save you and your loved ones a substantial sum of money. More important, you will be able to rest assured that you have found a plan that both carries out your wishes and protects your loved ones after your death.

What we have done for ourselves alone dies with us; what we have done for others and the world remains and is immortal.

—Albert Pike

PART I

THE NEED FOR ESTATE PLANNING AND ITS DEVELOPMENT

CHAPTER 1

The Need for Estate Planning

Learning Objectives

In this chapter, you will understand the need for estate planning as well as the following issues:

- Who needs to plan for an estate
- The options available to you in the estate-planning process
- The objectives of estate planning
- The key planning documents and how they are used
- The information required to plan an estate
- The major concerns in estate planning

Who Needs to Plan for an Estate?

You need an estate plan if:

- you are self-employed,
- you earn a salary as income,
- you are already a rich man,
- you are just there—neither rich nor poor,
- you are someone who earns a living, has an income, or owns property or investments—no matter how small.

Available Options for Planning

There are two basic options available to you if you decide to plan for your estate: you may plan *now, while still alive,* in a calm atmosphere while loads of naira-saving opportunities exist to choose from or you or your surviving spouse or family member (or even the state or local government!) *must* carry out the responsibility of distributing the estate immediately after a death during a period of emotional pain, sadness, and vulnerability when precious few naira-saving options remain or the naira available is not just enough anymore.

Basic Terms and Definitions

If you elect to commence the planning process while alive, it would be useful to understand all the concepts of estate planning.

What is a *plan*?

A plan is a methodical arrangement of specific steps necessary to get someone from where he currently is to where he desires to be. The fundamental rules that must be adhered to when attempting to make a plan are the following:

i. Establishing specific goals—what is your objective? Where are you going?

ii. Establishing your present position—where are you now in relation to that goal?

iii. Establishing a specific plan—by identifying and arranging to implement the specific steps that are necessary to bring you from your present position to your goal.

These basic rules of planning facilitate the six key stages of the planning process:

- gathering data (both qualitative and quantitative),
- establishing clear objectives as the estate owner,
- analyzing the data gathered,
- producing a comprehensive written estate plan with specific recommended actions to be taken,
- implementing the estate plan, and
- reviewing the estate plan periodically.

If you are thinking about creating your own estate plan, you should ask yourself:
"What am I really trying to achieve through planning for my estate, considering my own circumstance?"

Carefully thinking through this question will assist you to come to terms with what your goals should be when you decide to plan your estate. *Goal-oriented planning* should be the essence of any effort at preserving or retaining your estate.

What is an *estate*?

An estate is made up of a variety of different kinds of property, owned in one of several ways or having some type of interests attached to some of the property types. An estate describes the rights, titles, or interests that you have in property and refers to everything you own in your own name and your share of anything you own with other people.

If you no longer own property, it is out of your estate. Whatever you give away as a gift or sell belongs to the new owner.

What is *estate planning*?

The concept of estate planning is *"the process of acquiring, conserving, protecting, and distributing a person's property interests for the benefit of that person's heirs in the most effective and efficient manner consistent with maintaining that person's own financial independence and security."*

This means that estate planning enables you to effectively and efficiently attain the goals of accumulating wealth, ensuring that it is conserved, protected, and eventually distributed, after death, to beneficiaries chosen by that person. Essentially, therefore, it is about the processes followed when transferring property from one person to another, *especially* when such transfer is intended to take effect after the property owner's death.

It could therefore be deduced that these are the *core objectives* you intend to achieve when you decide to plan:

- to preserve your already accumulated wealth,
- to allow you use such wealth the way you desire during your lifetime,
- to pass on the greatest possible amount of your wealth to designated beneficiaries after you die,
- to ensure that you transfer your wealth and assets after your death as you wish,
- to plan for the proper transfer or disposal of closely held business interests,

- to decide who will be given the authority to settle the estate and how the estate is to be managed or administered.

However, several other estate-planning goals might exist that are personal and different to each individual estate planner. But that notwithstanding, the process of planning an estate hinges on two major components—the basic principles of planning for the distribution of an estate after the death of the owner and the selection of those methods of estate transfer that best suit the individual's *estate-planning objectives* and *financial situation.*

What is an *estate plan*?

An *estate plan* is a plan for the inevitable change of asset ownership that establishes how you can distribute your property interests both while alive and at death, according to your wishes. It also helps you to reduce the shrinkage of your estate in terms of its total value as a result of transfer expenses and taxes.

A good estate plan is created through the process of estate planning and is designed to bring your reality in line with your desires to the greatest extent possible.

Key Estate-Planning Documents

Every good estate plan is built upon the foundation of the essential estate-planning documents that cover all three phases of your life: while you are alive and well, if you become disabled, and after you die. A number of documents are required to take care of these life stages. But from the lot, five of them are important, depending on your current family and financial situation. They must be prepared—regardless of your age, health, and wealth—to be able to come up with a useful plan that would protect you and your property, as well as your family and loved ones.

These documents, explained briefly and in simple terms, are as follows:

1. Personal financial statement
   A personal financial statement is a formal record of a person's financial activities as an individual, and it consists of a single form for reporting personally held assets and liabilities (debts) or personal sources of income and expenses, or both.

2. Power of attorney
   A power of attorney is a document that appoints a person (called an "attorney") to act on behalf of another person who grants the power (the "donor") during the donor's lifetime.

   The purpose of a power of attorney is to provide proof of the attorney's powers. It allows the attorney to sign any document or do anything that the donor can do legally, subject to any conditions or limitations stated in the empowering document.

3. Will
   A will is a written legal document laying out clear and specific wishes of a person by way of instructions on how that person's property should be distributed, transferred, or managed after death.

4. Trust
   Trust is an arrangement that enables a person to transfer the legal title of property he owns to one person or entity while somebody else uses it or derives benefit from that same property.

5. Living will
   A living will is a revocable document that allows a person to state, *in advance*, what life-sustaining medical measures related to hydration, respiration, and nutrition should be taken by a health-care provider if that person (maker of the

living will), due to mental or physical incapacity, is unable to make decisions on what treatment is to be given.

Generally, a living will must be written, signed, and witnessed by persons who are not heirs or beneficiaries of the maker of the living will.

These documents represent planning techniques and should only be utilized within the framework of what they are able to achieve if you wish to plan efficiently and effectively.

Gathering Planning Information

An important step to take when preparing to commence your planning is to identify all the relevant information that would enable you to successfully set up a useful estate plan.

In order to do the best job possible, you will need to gather factual information about yourself and your assets. Your confirming that all the information so gathered are facts is critical because they will serve as the foundation for designing and implementing your estate plan.

The information needed could be classified into four categories:

i. Where you live
ii. What you own
iii. Who your beneficiaries are, and
iv. What your objectives are

Where You Live

This refers to your permanent home, and it is important because it determines the law that will govern the validity of your will and what it provides as well as how title to property is held. You must determine where exactly your domicile is before plans are formulated.

What You Own

A complete inventory of what you own must be gathered and may include assets like insurance policies, property owned jointly and separately, business interests, retirement and death benefits, claims under wills and trusts, and rights in future interests.

Also, the type of ownership you exercise over your property and assets—whether you own them in your name only or with some other person's name or through a company or whether your assets are subject to a claim by someone else (your wife or business partner)—is very useful. Information about your obligations must also be obtained—personal loans, business debts, accrued taxes, mortgages, leases, installment contracts, contingent liabilities, etc.

Who Your Beneficiaries Are

Facts concerning all the people that are your potential beneficiaries must be searched out and collated for the estate-planning purpose. Some of the useful information needed about them include the state of their health, age, wealth, and education and state of mental, physical, and emotional competency and character as well as their respective living needs.

Other useful information include the following:

- an evaluation of your responsibilities to your family,
- the business abilities of the potential beneficiaries,
- the wealth currently available to them,
- their financial needs,
- the attitudes they exhibit toward each other.

What Your Plan Planning Objectives Are

The goals you intend to achieve through planning your estate must be clear because determining your goals is critical for the development of an estate plan. It is very often *the most difficult phase* of gathering the facts.

In addition to gathering the above facts, you must determine and evaluate your existing estate plan. Most estate owners have an estate plan that they may have developed consciously or accidentally. When most of such owners have taken the trouble to make such evaluation and analyzed what they possess, they have been surprised at the results.

Reflections

1. What do you recall from this chapter
2. What emotions did you experience while reading through this chapter
3. Which aspect of this chapter held your attention the most
4. Which aspects of the chapter made sense to you based on your own circumstances
5. What issues would you focus on in your life after reading this chapter

CHAPTER 2

Estate Planning in Nigeria: The Evolution

Learning Objectives

At the end of this chapter, you would have a general overview of estate-planning activities in Nigeria and understand how the practice evolved.

Key aspects of the evolved practice include the following:

- The state of estate planning in ancient ethnic communities in Nigeria
- What communal estate planning is
- The doctrines and canons that dictated communal estate planning
- The specific canons of inheritance adopted and practiced by communities
- The influence of the colonialists on the Nigerian legal system

Before the Colonialists

The history of Nigeria clearly indicates that, long before the explorers from the British empire entered the territories that now make up what is now called Nigeria in the early part of the nineteenth century, more than 250 ethnic groups and communities with roots in those territories already had their respective communal customs and systems of traditional law in place, with established means of adjudicating justice for their people.

Some of the established customary practices and laws dealt with rights, obligations, and entitlements that made up core parts of the everyday living of those communities—such as marriage, divorce, work activities, property ownership, and death-time rituals. Examples of their rights included the holding, possession, ownership, transfer, or distribution of acquired wealth (both land and goods) as well as matters concerning succession to property, whether planned for or not.

Communal Estate Planning

A unique feature of the ethnic communities was the right they almost always reserved for themselves—collectively as communities—to prescribe customs and practices that must be adhered to by their people as it had to do with each person's rights to property as well as each person's obligations and entitlements. This was especially the case in matters of the distribution and ownership of property or estate by community members.

Most communities restricted the freedom or, in some extreme situations, outrightly denied their people the personal freedom to plan their own estates or even choose who their beneficiaries would be. Instead, the communities, as a collective, made those choices, decisions, and plans on their behalf through prescribed rules, guidelines, and custom-based laws that dictated how personal wealth—land or other property—

acquired by each individual would be succeeded, distributed, or inherited sometimes in their lifetimes but, mostly, after they pass on.

The ethnic groups to which property owners belonged, therefore, practiced a special type of planning that could be termed *communal estate planning*, which was distinct from estate planning carried out by individuals for their estates.

Attaining Goals

Communities used communal estate planning to plan the distribution and ownership of the estates of its individual members almost always without their personal input. The practice is long-entrenched and its goals remained, in general terms, similar to those of an individual who personally plans his estate—preserving and retaining wealth, property, or assets.

Communities used this prescriptive planning method, for instance, as a vehicle to facilitate property succession and gifting by their senior citizens and other property owners to succeeding generations of family members that would, otherwise, have been cumbersome or difficult to break up and distribute. Planning estates that way also helped to preserve family wealth and ensure the continuation of family-owned property on the incapacity or death of senior family members.

Other objectives of communal estate planning were to sustain social equilibrium within their communities and to promote and ensure social welfare as well as to maintain peace and order through ensuring their people's strict adherence to established property succession and inheritance laws.

Doctrines and Canons

Communal estate-planning practices in the various ethnic communities showed patterns that were as different as the more than 250 ethnic groups that existed, and continues to exist, in Nigeria. A strain of similarity among them, however, was certain foundational rules adopted and fused by most of them into their respective customary laws and practices. These rules, which governed property succession and inheritance, were called doctrines and canons.

The **doctrines of succession and inheritance** governed communal estate planning as the dominant mode of distributing and owning property or an estate. Canons of descent were rules adopted in determining who was eligible to inherit or succeed to the ownership of property—a next of kin as applicable to contemporary estate-planning matters.

By adopting these doctrines and canons in various formats that suited them, each ethnic community ensured, for instance, that property—especially land, a very important type of property in Nigerian communities—was inherited by, distributed to, or succeeded only by a small number of predetermined family members. That way, diffusion of ownership was almost completely avoided.

The most popular canons of descent infused into customary laws and practices with significant long-term impact on personal, family, and communal estates are the following:

- lines of inheritance,
- rule of primogeniture,
- taking per stirpes,
- taking per capita, and
- collateral heirs.

Lines of Inheritance

This canon of descent became a dominant rule that dovetailed to subsets of canons. These are the key ones:

i. Descending line of inheritance

   This subset canon of inheritance by lineage states that inheritance will descend or pass downward to the first child of a person who died last while in possession of the estate.

ii. Patrilineal line of inheritance

   The canon of patrilineal line of inheritance dictates that succession and inheritance of property in a family must only be through the children of a man.

   A significant percentage of ethnic communities South of Nigeria, including but not limited to the Bini, Onitsha, Itsekiri, Urhobo, Agbor, Ndokwa, Igbo-Ukwu, Agukwu-Nri, Owerre, Obowu, Wawa, Isiekeisi, Mbano, Mbaise, Mbaitolu, practice the canon of patrilineal inheritance.

iii. Inheritance by blood relationship

   The canon of inheritance by blood relationship states that only someone who is closest in degree of blood relationship inherits or succeeds to property, with men and boys always preferred over women and girls, and elder children always first in line over younger siblings.

   To accurately determine the relationship in order to ensure an acceptable succession to property, the proximity of the blood of the "heir(s)-to-be" to the property owner must be traced.

- Proximity of blood

  When determining the proximity of blood relationship between the property owner and a potential heir, the nature of the existing relationship is crucial. The relationship is of two kinds—**by consanguinity** and **by affinity**.

  Relationship by consanguinity is by blood, such as that of father and son, while relationship by affinity is that which arises by marriage, as husband and wife.

  The communities made it a rule that inheritance was only by consanguinity, never by affinity, either in ascending or descending line—such as father, mother, grandfather, grandmother, son, daughter, grandson, and granddaughter.

Rule of Primogeniture

One of the most popular canons of descent is the rule of primogeniture adopted by a significant number of ethnic communities in the Southern parts of the country, which states that *a firstborn son*—by law or custom—must inherit an entire estate, usually of a late parent or blood relations, to the exclusion of his younger siblings, male or female. The right of succession belongs to him and then to his own eldest son. Also, his direct descendants will take precedence over those of his siblings on inheritance matters.

The rule also states that older sons must be considered over younger sons and that all sons come first before any daughter in the family. Also, as children represent their late ancestors, the rule further prescribes that the senior line of descendants always comes first before the junior line of descent.

The rule of primogeniture is a powerful canon that is applied across several ethnic groups in the country. It is still being applied today as a very effective means of preventing the subdivision of estates as well as temptations to sell inherited property by an heir. Its effectiveness came from the accepted practice of polygamous marriages in most ethnic groups, through which property owners ensured that a son is produced from as many wives or concubines as possible.

In *Bini Kingdom*, the canon of primogeniture applies, and so the right to succession of the entire estate belongs exclusively to the eldest son of a deceased father, and he is expected to act as a sort of trustee for his siblings. The canon is so entrenched that even where the deceased father made an oral will, under Bini custom, the father will not be allowed to give the house where he lived and died in to any person other than his eldest son.

The rule of primogeniture has been intricately fused into the customary laws of large segments of *Igboland*, as well as in the lives of some *Efik communities.*

Taking Per Stirpes

Another canon applied in some of the communities is called *taking per stirpes.* With this canon, all descendants belonging to a particular line of ancestors are to stand in the same position—in terms of succession—as the property owner himself would have stood if he were alive.

"Standing in the same position" means that if there are three sons to inherit per stirpes but only two sons are alive, along with three children of the third deceased son, the two sons alone would take exactly what would have been due to them directly (one-third each), while the children of the late third son would each take one-third of their late father's third.

This canon was practiced in several parts of *Yoruba land* where distribution of an estate of a deceased husband and father who died intestate is per stirpes (known as *Idi Igi*), which means his estate got distributed on the basis of the number of wives he had and not by the number of his children.

Taking Per Capita

Taking per capita as a canon of descent means that the descendants of a deceased property owner will take the same shares of inheritance as those who stand in the same degree of relationship as the deceased property owner.

Therefore, if there are three sons to inherit but only two sons are alive, along with three children of the third deceased son, inheriting property by taking per capita would be that each living person would have one-fifth of the intestate's real property.

In the *Yoruba land situation* illustrated above, where a serious dispute erupts in the course of efforts to determine succession, the head of the family head is permitted, within some communities, to enforce his final discretion to distribute the deceased husband's estate by canon of taking per capital (called *Ori Ojori*) by the number of his children and not by the number of his wives.

Collateral Heirs

Yet another adopted canon in some of our customary laws is inheritance by collateral heirs. The canon provides that the collateral heir of a deceased property owner must be his next collateral kinsman of the whole blood. The determining factor for such collateral kinship is *whole blood.* This means that the heir and the property owner, who dies intestate, must be descendants from the same pair of ancestors.

By contrast, relationship by *half blood* is when there is only one common ancestor between them, as where the heir and deceased property owner are descendants of the same father but of different mothers. This type of relationship existed predominantly in polygamous family settings.

Where there are no children, the right to inherit passes to the collateral relatives in the order of seniority of the males of collateral lines. The eligible descendants of deceased elder siblings inherit first before living younger siblings.

Where property to be succeeded is *ancestral land of a family*, only collateral heirs of the whole blood are eligible to inherit such. However, collateral heirs of the half-blood may be eligible to inherit lands not deemed to be from ancestral descent, although they most often end up taking fewer shares than whole-blood heirs.

In *Idomaland* and *Yorubaland* respectively, collateral heirs of the whole blood applied as neither a husband nor a wife could inherit one another's property, especially land, as they are not related by blood. If the wife dies without bearing a child, her property gets distributed to her siblings.

On the other hand, people of the *Kalabari* and *Netembe* ethnic kingdoms practiced inheritance by collateral heirs of the half-blood where, under their Iya marriage custom, a wife, in addition to her children from her husband, have the right to inherit his property.

Some Igbo communities practiced these canons of collateral heirs, either wholly or as varied, as they suited the cultural beliefs of their respective clans and lineages.

In addition to the canons mentioned above, some communities adopted and practiced other canons that were not so popular, but which suited their lifestyles and belief system. The most common of the canons are as follows:

- Matrilineal line of inheritance
- Rule of ultimogeniture

Matrilineal Line of Inheritance

The canon subset of matrilineal succession prescribed the practice of a man's property and wealth inherited by his sister's children and his own children being the heirs of their mother's brothers (maternal uncles).

This canon of inheritance is practiced by the Abiriba, Ohafia, and Item communities in Igboland in the present day. Consequently, their communities place a premium on their daughters marrying within their communities, although sons who desire to marry girls from outside their communities are not discouraged.

Rule of Ultimogeniture

The canon of ultimogeniture prescribes the order of succession to property to be that the youngest son (or youngest child) succeeds the dead estate owner. The rule has proved useful in circumstances where the youngest, for instance, elects to stay at home to care for the parents, while the older children have chosen to pursue success "out in the world" and provide for themselves.

As unpopular as this canon appeared to be among ethnic communities, it still got adopted and practiced by the Markis group of the Verbe community of Northern Nigeria. Here, the youngest son inherits to the total exclusion of any other potential heir of the deceased estate owner.

The Coming of the Colonialists

The arrival of the British colonial rule on the shores of the territories that subsequently evolved to the nation-state named Nigeria had tremendous impact on the established ways of life of the indigenous communities that already lived there. The eventual impact of their coming on Nigeria's legal system has led to the operation, side by side, of three different systems of law, namely:

- English common law
- Nigerian statutory laws
- Customary laws (including Islamic laws)

English common law is made up of an accumulated body of cases decided in the courts of Britain, including cases decided before the year 1900. The English common law applies till today in the country, some with substantial modifications by Nigerian statutes.

Nigerian statutory laws are essentially English statutory laws that have been accepted by Nigeria and restated in the laws of the country through reenactments or amendments, as well as fresh or original laws made by Nigerian legislative authorities.

Customary laws comprise the body of rules and practices governing particular groups of people in Nigerian communities. It includes Islamic laws, which are religious tenets that dictate the ways of life of people of the Islamic faith.

The application of this rather unique three-tier legal system, sometimes referred to as legal pluralism, in estate-planning matters—personal and communal—sometimes leads to serious and very complex consequences for the people concerned. It was difficult—in many situations that had to do with distribution and ownership of estates—to determine who could exercise the rights to inherit or succeed to property. Over time, however, an effective rule that assisted in resolving what law should be applied in matters of estate administration evolved. The rule is this: *Did the estate owner make a will?*

Reflections

1. What historical information in this chapter do you think is relevant
2. What was your gut response to all that you read about
3. What were the benefits and downsides of the doctrines and canons explained
4. What viable options are available to people and communities now
5. What do you need to verify from this chapter

CHAPTER 3

Communal Planning for Intestacy

Learning Objectives

At the end of this chapter, you would have grasped the following issues:

- Intestate distribution under customary laws
- The impact of marriage on intestacy
- How property types determine property distribution on intestacy
- General tenets of Islamic law of inheritance

Choosing to Die Intestate

If a person dies without making a valid will, he is said to have died intestate. A valid will under customary law includes a set of oral instructions on how a person's estate must be succeeded or distributed when death occurs.

The concept of communal estate planning, as discussed extensively in chapter 2, completely captures intestate distribution of property under customary law. It is almost a norm for estate owners in ethnic communities not only to do away with personally planning their estates before they die but to let their whole lives, and death, be dictated by the customs and cultural practices laid down by their respective communities.

Expanded Criteria

Nigeria's postcolonial three-tier legal system has led to slightly more complex criteria for the application of customary law to the estate of a person who dies intestate. The simple criterion originally was just that the person must be a member of the ethnic community applying those customary practices or that he must have lived the life of a devout Muslim to enable Islamic tenets on property inheritance be applied on all that he owns.

However, the country's legal pluralism led to the criteria being expanded to include the following:

- The person must be subject to customary law;
- If the person married a wife under the Nigerian Marriage Act, he would have died after *the death* his wife or child by that marriage surviving him; and
- He must have conducted that Act marriage in Nigeria and nowhere else.

If any of the above criteria is not met, statutory laws or the English common law *will almost automatically* replace customary law, as the law to apply to the intestate property, without regard as to how that would affect the person's estate.

Impactful Canons

The canons of descent had a fundamental impact on the way estates were succeeded or distributed as well as how the eligibility of beneficiaries were determined. The most popular canons adopted were the rule of primogeniture and inheritance by proximity of blood.

A review of how these canons impacted customary intestate distribution of property are illustrated below:

i. Distribution of estate on a proximity of blood basis(consanguinity)

   - A woman is not eligible to inherit land from her father or brothers within the Edo and Ishan (Esan) communities although she can receive other property types such as domestic animals, cooking utensils, fruit trees, and clothes from their estate.

   - The Igbo community declares a woman not qualified to inherit land from her own family, as property passes from a father to his first son. If she is not yet married, she has the right to live in her father's house; but the minute she marries, that right is lost.

   - An Hausa woman takes a share in the distribution of property in their custom. She is entitled to be given half of the shares that go to the men in her family. However, in current practice, if she ends up as her father's only surviving child, she will succeed all proceeds from a farmland but relinquish the right to occupy her father's land to her uncle who then succeeds as of right in that circumstance. This development is a consequence of the increasing pressure on land all over the country.

- In Yoruba land, no distinction is made between males and females when estates are being distributed. Both men and women get to inherit property within their own families—parents, brothers, and sisters. However, what women contend with when they marry and leave their families are contests of their rights to inherited property by the men in their families.

ii. Distribution of estate on a proximity of blood basis(affinity)

- In Adamawa State, the Hausa and Fulani communities distribute the property of a dead intestate man who was married equally between his widow and his parents.

- In most Igbo communities, a woman cannot inherit land from her husband's estate, as his family takes such as family land and a birthright not to be passed to an outsider. She can only inherit through a male child she may have with her husband, if that child accepts to give her a part of the property. If a woman acquires property jointly with her husband, she still will not have the right to inherit that property, even when proven.

- In the Ijaw community of South-Southern Nigeria, a woman cannot inherit from her husband's property because they practice the canon of descent that prescribes the succession to estate property by consanguineous proximity of blood.

- In Hausa land, its customary law recognizes the right of a woman to inherit from her husband's estate even if she is childless. That practice helps bolster patrilineal inheritance of cattle, with the woman assured of care and protection long after the husband's death.

- In Igbo land, as well as in some communities found in parts of Delta and Edo states, a man cannot inherit his wife's share of her own family property as the man is deemed to be a stranger to her family and therefore not entitled to share in the family property of which he is not a member.

iii. Distribution of estate on the basis of collateral heirs

- Among the Igbo, when the only child of a man is female (girl or woman), his estate passes to the oldest male relation in his family. To qualify, that oldest man must be related to this woman's father through a common blood ancestor.

- The estate of a dead intestate man is accepted in some Yoruba communities to be distributable only among his children, to the exclusion of all other relatives.

iv. Distribution on the basis of the primogeniture rule

- In most of the Igbo, Bini, and Urhobo communities, family land or compound is always reserved for the eldest son who is entitled to a large share of it while the other siblings divide the rest in diminishing proportions, if at all.

A more detailed look at the impact of some of the fused canons of inheritance in two ethnic communities in Nigeria is illustrated by the cases below:

Case Studies

1. The Itsekiri Community of Delta State

Traditionally, where a deceased man has children from more than one wife/line, his estate is shared according to the number of fruitful wives. Childless wives are not entitled to anything. But if the childless wives chose to remain in the family, they could be given some portion of the estate. The different "lines" share their portions among themselves. Generally, daughters get a larger share of cash portion of the estate to compensate them for not being entitled to sown clothes from their fathers' estates.

Wives are regarded as part of a man's estate and are shared among the male children that are old enough to marry. Where there are no grown-up sons, the women are shared among the junior brothers of the deceased or relations in the absence of brothers. Where a woman refuses to be shared, a male member of the family of the husband is made to walk across her stretched-out legs in the presence of the family as a symbol of her release or freedom.

The eldest son of the dead man succeeds his father's residence. Where the deceased man has no children, his estate is shared among his junior siblings, male and female.

In the case of women, her estate is shared among her children. Where there are no children, sharing is among her junior siblings.

However, the custom has been modified such that today, the sharing of a deceased man's estate is extended beyond the number of wives that bore children for him to include his brothers and sisters as well as the wife (wives) with no issues who chooses to remain in the family.

Wives can also be given to their own children, irrespective of whether they are male or female. Wives could be inherited by their sisters and brothers. In any of these cases, males within the family hierarchy of the deceased would be made to walk across the out-stretched legs of the widow and perform symbolic traditional marital rites in public glare.

However, the sharing of a deceased's estate, including the widows, takes place only on completion of all funeral rites.

2. The Igbomina Community Located within Osun and Kwara States

The Igbomina community is an extension of the Yoruba ethnic community living in parts of Osun and Kwara States of Nigeria. Their community is structured in cells, a system they call Ebi—an extended family structure evolving from about four generations. An Ebi represents a family clan with the eldest among the clan usually designated its head and known as Olori Ebi.

Within this cell structure, an association of ten or more Ebi is called a compound (Agbo Ile). The Agbo Ile is led by an Olori Ile (head of the compound). The two leaders play a vital role in the distribution of estate in line with their customary practices.

In Igbomina, distribution or inheritance is governed by the Yoruba customary law, but some estate owners who were practicing Muslims get to have Islamic law take effect on their estates.

In Yoruba customary law, the general rule is that both the male and female children, entitled to succeed their father's property on his death intestate, share equally per capita (Ojo Ori) or per stirpes (Idi Igi), where the man left behind more than one wife. This law applies to estates in the community.

However, if the man made a verbal declaration or a written commitment before his death as to how he preferred that his estate be distributed and if this can be attested to by not less than three persons, in this case, the olori ebi assumes the role as the administrator and the head of the distribution team; in which case he is not able to execute this role due to ill health, the olori ile or the next in age to either of them acts on his behalf.

Also, the Igbomina community agrees with the practice of men automatically succeeding to their late wives' estate, unlike most of the other communities discussed earlier. Where their wives do not have husbands surviving them, the estates get transferred to her husband to their children.

Islamic Law of Inheritance

Whether Islamic law applies to determine the rights of inheritance to a dead person's estate as opposed to his customary law within some communities in Nigeria does not rest merely on the premise that the dead estate owner was known to be a Muslim.

The critical condition to apply Islamic law is that, in addition to having accepted the Islamic faith, the dead person must have lived his life and conducted his affairs in accordance with Islamic injunctions. The intestate must also have shown a clear intention to be bound by Islamic law. If that is found not to be the case, customary law will apply in distributing his assets.

The power to pass on inheritance in Islamic law is limited to one-third of the estate. The remaining two-thirds of the estate is distributed among the heirs according to the prescribed positions(called *fasaid*) after settlement of debts such as charges on land property, unpaid purchase price, and funeral or interment expenses.

The predominant Islamic faith in Nigeria is the Maliki School, and as explained by some Islamic scholars of that faith, succession rights practiced by its faith community are mathematically laid out in the Qur'an.

The Maliki School recognizes three basic canons of inheritance:

- Marriage under a valid contract in Islamic law
- Consanguinity, i.e., the blood relationship between the deceased and heirs, including ascendants and descendants, siblings, uncles, aunts
- Clientship personal relationship between an emancipated slave and his emancipator.

They explained that, as stipulated by the Islamic tenets of inheritance, their acknowledged primary heirs and their shares are the following:

- a father—one-sixth (1/6) of the estate
- a grandfather—one-sixth (1/6)
- a mother—one-sixth (1/6) with a child and one-third (1/3) if she is without a child
- a grandmother—one-sixth (1/6) with a child and, without a child, one-third (1/3)
- a husband—one-fourth (1/4) with a child and half (1/2) of the estate, without a child
- a wife or wives—one-eighth (1/8) with a child and one-fourth (1/4) without a child

In recent times, however, Islamic jurisprudence has been known to accept the notion that inheritance should be limited strictly to people related to the late estate owner by blood and marriage.

Limitations to Customary Intestate Distribution

Despite the deeply rooted intestate distribution practice in all the ethnic communities, there are some exceptions to the rule that customary canons of inheritance govern intestacy. These exceptions include the following:

- Oral declaration of the dead estate owner
- Family verdict
- Application by the court of rules of natural justice
- Change of "cultural" status through marriage
- Recognized evolutionary process of customary law.

Oral Declaration

Customary law is flexible and adaptable to changes in the patterns of life of people in any ethnic community. There are instances where a person chooses to orally prescribe—before his death and in the presence of mature and responsible family members—how he wants his property and wealth to be distributed or succeeded and who he wants as a beneficiary of his estate.

Such a person may have upheld his community's particular culture and canons of inheritance of estate throughout his lifetime but, for reasons best known to him, has decided to go against those customary prescriptions and disinherited specific individual(s) from his estate.

When this happens, the intention of that person, when proved, takes priority over any customary law when he dies, as his oral declaration is taken as his will.

Family Verdict

Family verdict is sometimes applied in waiving the application of communal estate planning when a person dies intestate, especially for purposes of distributing his estate equitably to all his surviving family members. This verdict is reached in wisdom by a family in consensus by all or a significant majority and is of great significance where applying the rules of customary law will cause great hardship or disagreement among members of the family.

Rules of Natural Justice

As most laws and practices of estate inheritance and distribution are embedded in the culture of ethnic communities, the laws may, over time, be found to be out of touch with new thinking or new ways of doing things by contemporary society.

The consequences of applying some of the customary laws of intestate distribution of estate on the surviving family members of the dead intestate property owner could be so obnoxious as to be against the rules of natural justice, equity, and good conscience. In such situations, the courts have been relied upon to take decisions to correct identified anomalies by directing alternative estate distribution methods or rules.

New Cultural Status through Marriage

When women marry under customary practice, they assume the culture of their husbands and, by that, adopt new status in their new communities. In most cases, their marriages mean that the communal laws and practices apply to them as well. Where there are differences in the rules of estate distribution between the customs of their fathers and those of their husbands, the latter take precedence.

Evolving Customary Process

The customary law of an ethnic group or community represents all its beliefs, lifestyle, faith, social structure, property ownership, and much more. Developments, as life progresses, could be so rapid that customs and cultural practices once held sacrosanct could, in short periods, turn to being archaic and no longer practicable.

Such evolution in customary laws, once recognized wholly by communities, result to changes in rules applicable to them; this way, the change comes from within the community, as opposed to a change imposed by courts or from an outside influence or event.

Case Study

Here is a recent example of how far the customary law of a Nigerian could affect his personal situation, even outside the country.

Nigerian Oil Tycoon to Fight £17m Divorce with Itsekiri Customary Law (even though he built his fortune in the United Kingdom, his wife is British, and they lived together in London).

> *Michael Prest, a wealthy Nigerian-born, British-based oil tycoon has been granted permission to use Nigerian customary law to appeal a #17million divorce payout to his former British wife. Prest, the 50 year-old founder of Nigerian energy trading company, Petrodel Resources, split from his wife in an acrimonious divorce in 2008.*
>
> *During a British High Court hearing on the divorce in October last year, the presiding judge ordered the tycoon to pay his former wife cash and assets worth over #17.5million. He was also ordered to pay maintenance of #24,000 a year for each of his four children, along with their private school fees and medical bills.*

However, Prest has applied to appeal the court's decision on the grounds that his Petrodel's assets do not belong to him but are held in trust for his children, siblings, nephews and nieces in Nigeria under Nigerian Itsekiri customary law.

The Oil Tycoon claimed that his company, Petrodel Resources Limited, was established in 1992 with #10,000 in start-up capital which was given to him by his late father. His lawyer, Martin Pointer, disclosed to the court that under Itsekiri customary law in Nigeria, Prest, being the first born son of his family, became head of the family after his father's death with a traditional responsibility to use the family "inheritance" to look after his siblings and their children.

Prest's case is also helped by the fact that his younger brother, Michel, went to a Nigerian High Court in 2009 and obtained a declaration which stated that Petrodel Resources Limited is a part of their late father's estate. Michael Prest also previously obtained a court order from another Nigerian court which forbade him sharing information about Petrodel and its assets with third parties. As a result, it became difficult to ascertain the true market value of the company.

Mrs. Yasmin Prest, his former wife, had argued in the original High Court divorce case last October, that her former husband was worth 'many tens, if not hundreds, of millions of pounds', that Petrodel is '100 per cent owned and controlled' by him and that the company was effectively his 'alter ego'. She had been seeking a payout of more than £30million, plus more than £730,000 a year for her and her children to meet their reasonable needs. Prest had offered her £27,000 a year and a lump sum of less than £2million. He claimed to have had no regular income for more than a year.

The court heard Mrs. Prest was born in England and grew up on the Isle of Man. She met Prest, who was educated in Nigeria, in London and they married in 1993. They lived in a £4million home in Bayswater, west London, and the oldest of their children is 14. An £11.3million London property portfolio was also built up, with almost all the flats and houses being owned by one of Prest's numerous companies.

Prest, who was named as one of the three most influential black men in Britain in 2007, argued that the Isle of Man–based company, Petrodel Resources should not have been included when assessing his ex-wife's award. Several of Prest's companies, including Petrodel Resources, are also appealing the divorce payout in their own rights.

Lord Justice Thorpe said: 'The ownership of Petrodel is bound up with Nigeria and may be governed by customary law.'

The family court hearing could not be reported, but details of the multi-million-pound divorce battle could now be disclosed as the case has gone to the Appeal Court, which is not subject to the same blanket reporting restrictions. No date has been set for the full appeal. Michael Prest, an extremely reclusive figure, has managed to keep a low public profile despite achieving huge success in the oil business. He became a successful oil trader before founding Petrodel Resources Limited in 2001.

(Adapted from http://www.dailymail.co.uk/news/article-2103792/Oil-tycoon-Michael-Prest-use-African-customary-native-law-claim-17-5m-divorce-payout-back.html#ixzz21eux1SiX and Mfonobong Nsehe, a Forbes blogs contributor)

Reflections

1. What words or phrases do you recall from this chapter
2. What were the high points and low points of this chapter for you
3. What information did you struggle with
4. What new perspective has this chapter given you
5. What steps would you take to explore what you learnt from the chapter

CHAPTER 4

Statutes of Intestacy

Learning Objectives

By the end of this chapter, you should be able to understand how Nigerian legislations and the common law provide for estate succession where a will has not been written. Issues include the following:

- Intestate distribution under statutory laws
- How the three-tier legal system affects intestacy
- The impact of marriage on intestacy
- The statutory distribution of estates on basis of property types

Estates and a Three-Tier Legal System

It could be taken that while the matter of estate planning under Nigerian statutory laws has, to a significant degree, provided clarity, the customary law doctrine of succession and ownership of property remain generally unpredictable.

In the midst of the three-tier legal system, the possibility of easing the troubles encountered by people concerned with the succession to the estate of family members, relatives, and loved ones became a bit more realizable through asking a key question:

> "Did the estate owner make a will before dying?"

The response to this question helps determine which of the three parallel laws to apply in each situation. If the deceased estate owner made a will, he would be taken to have died testate. If, on the other hand, he did not make any will before dying or his will turned out to be invalid, he died intestate.

Once it has been clearly established that he made a will—confirmed to meet all the criteria of a valid will as stated by the relevant laws—Nigerian statutory laws on wills, as it relates to the deceased's particular circumstance, will apply. If no such laws exist, common law principles on wills become applicable in distributing his estate.

If, however, it turns out that he died without making a will, a different question arises as the state of intestacy brings up more concerns. Ultimately, the question that would help to resolve the issue of inheritance is this:

> "Was the estate owner, who died without a will, a person to whom statutory laws or customary laws applied during his lifetime?"

If the response to this question is that the dead intestate estate owner was a person who, in his lifetime, had statutory laws applying to him, then the provisions of the relevant Nigerian laws on administration of estates would apply to his estate. If there are no enacted Nigerian laws, the common law on intestate death will be used in distributing his property.

Where the question posed confirms that, in the lifetime of the intestate owner, only customary laws applied to him as a person, then his estate would be distributed in line with the canons of descent practiced by his ethnic community or his Islamic community, if it is confirmed that he practiced the faith.

Asking these crucial questions help to navigate the challenging situation of legal pluralism in Nigeria as far as the administration of intestate estates is concerned.

> "When a person dies without making a valid will, what happens to his or her estate?"

Estate Planning Freedom

A significant impact that the coming of the colonialists had on existing practices of property succession and distribution in Nigeria was the substantial freedom granted to individuals to personally plan their own estates through the introduction of the English common laws and statutes into the country's legal system.

One of the important benefits of owning property is the right to decide how to dispose of it as one desires during a lifetime and at death. A person's life and death thus provide opportunities to transfer his property to another in a variety of ways that he alone will exercise control over. One of these ways is by making a will.

The personal freedom to carry out estate planning in the country could be traced to the English Statute of Frauds of 1677, as it was the first attempt at providing in writing what was required to utilize a will for the distribution of a person's own property. That statute streamed its way into our legal system through the adopted English common law and its influence on local laws. It attempted to bar communal estate planning from applying to people's estates and gave them liberty to personally determine how their estates were to be distributed as well as the right to choose who their beneficiaries would be.

Despite the new freedom given, most people neglect or fail to write a will before they pass on. When that happens, all that a person owns—his estate—will be distributed according to the rules of estate administration governing intestacy, whether or not he would have wanted the rules to apply to his estate were he still alive. This is so because he failed or neglected to make such a choice in his lifetime when he had the opportunity.

The State v. The Person

Two different rules of estate administration apply to estates on intestacy, and they are based on statutory laws and customary laws. Ascertaining which of the two rules to apply to the estate of a person who died intestate depends on that person's particular circumstance—whether the person is subject to statutory laws or the customary laws of his ethnic community. His customary law is also referred to as his *personal law*.

If it is determined that the dead intestate person was subject to statutory laws during his lifetime, his estate will be administered in line with the provisions of any relevant Nigerian law dealing with the administration of estates where he lived or where his estate is located. Where no such law exists or none enacted yet, common law will be applied.

When Statutes Apply on Intestacy

When a person dies intestate, he loses his right to choose how his property will be divided or inherited. He has no voice when the statutes are utilized to administer his estate, as the relevant law will empower the courts to determine who will administer his estate instead. That way, the statutes create an estate plan on his behalf.

The three laws that applied to intestacy were the following:

- Common law—the rule in *Cole v. Cole*
- The Nigerian Marriage Act—Section 36
- The Administration of Estates Law of Lagos State and Western Nigeria—Section 49 (5)

The English common law applied to intestate estates in the absence of Nigerian laws dealing with intestacy. When laws eventually got enacted in some parts of Nigeria for the administration of estates, it created the three-tier legal system that allows common law and statutes to operate simultaneously in addition to customary laws.

A basic grasp of what they were about and the consequences of each law will illustrate the impact that intestacy had, and continues to have, on the lives of Nigerians.

Common Law—The Rule in *Cole v. Cole*

The decision of the court in the common law case of *Cole v. Cole* (decided in 1898) was the first time in recorded history that marriage was highlighted as a very important factor when determining what estate administration laws would apply to the estate of a person who left no valid will.

In that case, Cole, a native of Lagos, lived most of his life in Lagos and died there as well.

During his lifetime, he contracted a Christian marriage with one Mary Cole in Sierra Leone and they both had one child called Alfred Cole. When Cole died in 1897, his brother, A. B. Cole, brought an action claiming to be declared the customary heir of the late Cole, according to their customary law.

Cole's widow resisted this claim on the ground that the succession to Cole's estate was to be governed by English law and not customary law. Under English law, the widow and son were entitled to inherit the estate to the exclusion of the brother.

In arriving at a decision, the Full Court considered section 14 of the Supreme Court Ordinance of 1876 which provided that:

"The common law, the doctrines of equity, and the statues of general application which were in force in England at the date when the Colony obtained a local legislature" *were to be in force throughout the Colony.*

The court also considered section 19 of the Ordinance which provided that:

"No party shall be entitled to claim the benefit of any local law or custom if it shall appear, either from express contract or from the nature of the transactions out of which any suit on question may have arisen, that such party agreed that his obligations in connection with the transactions should be regulated exclusively by English law and in cases where no express rule is applicable to any matter in controversy, the court shall be governed by the principles of justice, equity, and good governance."

At the end of its deliberations, the Court decided that by getting into a Christian marriage, which meant having one wife, Cole

> *had removed his estate from being ruled by his community's customary laws of estate succession and distribution, to the English Common law system.*

Adapted from *Nigerian Law of Succession (Principles, Cases, Statutes, and Commentaries)* by Itse Sagay

The Marriage Factor

The decision in *Cole v. Cole* set out what could be termed "the canons of determination" subsequently adopted as a way of finding out which statute applied to an intestate property. To determine what canon to apply, the question to ask is this:

> "What type of marriage did the dead intestate person get into when he was alive?"

The Nigerian Marriage Act

The Marriage Act, which was enacted in 1958 as part of the laws of the country, was the main statute that laid out laws governing marriages conducted in Nigeria. It, therefore, had significant impact on the estate of any person who got married according to its prescriptions.

Its impact on intestacy arose from its **Section 36**, which stated that:

> *"Where any person subject to Customary law contracted a marriage under the Act, and such a person died intestate, leaving a spouse or issue of such a marriage, all his property, both real and personal, would be distributed according to the English law relating to the distribution of personal property of an intestate."*

This provision of Section 36 meant that, even where a person's customary or personal law applied exclusively to his life circumstance, if he goes ahead to marry a wife according to the prescriptions of the Marriage Act of 1958 and subsequently dies without making a will for his estate, all his property will be distributed according to the decision in the English case of *Cole v. Cole*. This was so despite the existence of the Marriage Act itself, a Nigerian statute.

The East of Nigeria

Section 36 and the decision taken in the case of *Cole v. Cole* applied for a long time to intestate estates of persons who were subject to statutory laws in Eastern Nigeria. However, growing dissatisfaction with the consequences of those laws led three states in Eastern Nigeria—Anambra, Ebonyi, and Enugu—to enact the Administration and Succession (Estate of Deceased Persons) Law, 1987. That law was previously known as the Succession Edict 1987 of old Anambra State.

The 1987 law made specific provisions under its Section 120, which, in summary, stated exactly how the estate of a dead intestate person should be succeeded by his survivors. In all its provisions, the law made it clear that where a wife survives her spouse, her succession to his estate was only till her own death or till she remarries.

The law also adopted some canons of descent, such as the proximity of blood and consanguinity, in determining who should succeed an intestate's estate.

The Rest of Nigeria

- Rivers State

Rivers State was an integral part of the former Eastern Nigeria region, and so the laws that applied to that region was operational in the state. However, in 1999, the government established the Administration of Estate Law, Cap 1, Laws of Rivers State of Nigeria 1999, which effectively took the state out of the rule in *Cole v. Cole.*

- Abia, Akwa Ibom, Bayelsa, Cross River and Imo States, and the Northern States

With nonlegislation in the other Eastern States of Abia and Imo as well as all of Northern Nigeria, till date, of specific laws dealing with the estate of a home-born Nigerian who marries under the existing marriage laws in Chapter 218, Laws of the Federal Republic of Nigeria, and dies without a will but leaves behind a wife or child, the rule in *Cole v. Cole* still applies to statutory intestacy in those parts of the country.

Western Nigeria

The application of Section 36 to Nigerian intestates caused so many difficulties, pain, and other awful outcomes that it was labelled an obnoxious piece of legislation in many quarters. Specifically, the Western region of Nigeria went ahead to abolish the application of that Section 36, as well as the English common law–decided case of *Cole v. Cole* in their region by enacting the Administration of Estates Law of Western Nigeria in 1959.

Lagos State

As a federal territory at the time, up until the independence of Nigeria in 1960, Lagos was bound to apply all laws enacted by the central government of Nigeria. The Marriage Act and its dreaded Section 36 was one of those laws.

However, soon after Lagos was formally created as a State of its own in 1967, its government set out to review all laws that were effective there, in the course of which Section 36 got taken out completely from its laws. In its place, the State chose to extend the application of the Administration of Estates Law of Western Nigeria to Lagos through a new law—the Applicable Laws Edict of 1972. With that move, the decision in *Cole v. Cole* based on English common law principles as well as Section 36 of the Marriage Act stopped applying to intestacy in Lagos State.

Currently, the Administration of Estates Law is captured in Chapter 1 of the Laws of Lagos State, 1994.

The Administration of Estates Law of Lagos State and Western Nigeria

The decision of Western Nigeria, including Lagos State, to rewrite the destiny of their citizens with respect to intestacy was captured by the words of Section 49 (5) of their Administration of Estates Law, which stated that:

> *"Where any person who is subject to customary law contracts a marriage in accordance with the provisions of the Marriage Ordinance, and such a person dies intestate after the commencement of this law leaving a widow or husband or any issue of such marriage, any property of which the said intestate might have disposed of by Will, shall be distributed in accordance with the provisions of this law, any customary law to the contrary notwithstanding."*

Preliminary Conditions

Section 49 (5) was, therefore, clear that specific conditions must exist or be met for the statute to apply to any given intestate situation. These conditions were that:

i. The law applied to anyone living in Lagos State and the old Western States who was *not* subject to customary law, regardless of the type of marriage such a person contracted.

ii. The dead intestate person must have opted to marry under the Marriage Act, even though he is subject to customary law.

iii. The dead intestate person must be survived by a spouse or child of such a marriage.

iv. Estate properties covered by Section 49 (5) were those that the deceased could have distributed himself through a written will.

Implications

The implications of the conditions required to exist or be met before the Administration of Estates Law could apply were as follows:

- The presence of a spouse or child *of a marriage conducted under the Marriage Act* only sets off the application of this law.
- Under this law, a wife married under customary law is recognized as a wife when it is time to distribute the estate of the dead owner (husband) who dies without a will.
- Where an estate owner who is subject to customary or personal law dies intestate without a surviving wife or a child who was a product of his statutory marriage with that wife, his estate will be distributed according to his customary law.
- The condition of having married under the Marriage Act before the Administration of Estates law came into being affected only intestate Nigerians who are subject to customary law.

- That law did not apply to Nigerians who, being subject to their customary or personal laws, also contracted monogamous Christian marriages outside Nigeria.
- The law did not apply to family property, as the intestate dead person could not have distributed such a property himself by his will.

What Type of Property?

The three-tier legal system has put in place general rules that must be followed when determining how to distribute or succeed the estate of a dead intestate person. These rules are based primarily on the type of property comprising such an intestate estate. The question that helps to give clarity is this:

"Is the estate property to be distributed a movable or immovable type?"

The statutory rules are as follows:

Movable Property

a. The laws of the place where the estate owner died are used to determine how his movable property will be distributed or inherited.

b. If the property of the intestate person is movable and he died in any of the western states of Oyo, Ogun, Osun, Ondo, Ekiti, and Lagos (and which includes Edo and Delta states), the Administration of Estates Law will be used as a guide to distributing them, regardless of where the property is located.

c. If the intestate person died in any of the eastern or northern states of Nigeria and his estate is comprised of movable property, the existing laws of the state where he died will apply, without regard to where those properties have been kept.

Immovable Property

d. The laws operating where his immovable property (which is almost always land) is located guide the succession to that property.

e. If the intestate's immovable property being administered is located in any of the western states of Oyo, Ogun, Osun, Ondo, Ekiti, and Lagos, or within the former midwestern states of Edo and Delta States, it will be succeeded or distributed in line with the provisions of the Administration of Estate Laws. The only condition to be met, however, is that the immovable property itself must not be subject to customary law.

f. If the immovable property is located within any of the eastern or northern states, the English common law decision in *Cole v. Cole* will apply. The consequence is straightforward—the person's heir succeeds that property.

General

g. If the intestate person was married under customary law alone at the time he died, only customary law will apply to his estate distribution. If he was not married at all or he got married under the Marriage Act but had no surviving child from that marriage, his estate will also be distributed according to his customary law.

h. Despite all the above rules, circumstances may come up requiring that an estate's movable property be distributed under one law and the immovable property under a separate law.

A Summary

Listed below is a summary of the effects that the emphasis laid on the marriage factor by the judges in the case of *Cole v. Cole* had on a wide variety of intestate situations in Nigeria:

i. If the dead intestate person entered a Christian marriage outside Nigeria and, by that, had only one spouse in his lifetime, his estate will be administered by English common law;

ii. If the dead intestate person married under the provisions of the Marriage Act of Nigeria— a statutory law—and then died while living either in Lagos or within the boundaries of the old western region (made up of Oyo, Ogun, Osun, Ondo, Ekiti, Edo and Delta States)of Nigeria, his estate will be distributed according to the laws enacted for estate administration in that region;

iii. If, while still married, as recognized by the Marriage Act, the person dies intestate while living in any of the states that made up the former Northern region (Abuja, Adamawa, Bauchi, Benue, Borno, Nasarawa, Jigawa, Kaduna, Kano, Katsina, Kebbi, Kogi, Kwara, Niger, Plateau, Taraba, Yobe, Zamfara) or the Eastern regions (Abia, Anambra, Ebonyi, Enugu and Imo States) of Nigeria, English common law will be deployed in distributing his estate. This is because these regions are yet to enact statutory laws specifically for estate administration.

iv. If the person was a native-born Nigerian and did not conduct a Christian marriage that is subject to the Marriage Act when he was alive, his customary or personal law would be the basis of the distribution of his estate.

v. Even if such a person entered into a Christian marriage that is recognized by the Marriage Act but had no wife or no child from that marriage as surviving family members after his death, his customary or personal law will still apply to his estate.

vi. If the person lived his life as a Muslim, then Islamic law and its tenets on inheritance of property will govern the estate he left behind.

Reflections

1. What words or phrases do you recall from this chapter

2. What emotions did you experience while reading through this chapter

3. What were some of the issues raised in your mind concerning the different conditions and implications of the Administration of Estates Law of Lagos and Western States

4. What aspect of the chapter comes close to the situation in your culture

5. How, in your view, should the complex consequences of statutory intestacy be ameliorated

I am ready to meet my maker but, whether my maker is prepared for the great ordeal of meeting me is another matter.

—Winston Churchill

PART II

THE ESSENTIALS OF MODERN ESTATE PLANNING

CHAPTER 5

Understanding Property

Learning Objectives

After reading this chapter, you should be able to understand the fundamental issues of estate planning such as:

- How property is understood in estate planning
- The basic kinds of property
- Forms of property ownership
- The various ways to transfer property

Property at the Center of Estate Planning

In Nigeria, most, if not all, of the ethnic groups, distinct communities, and clusters of people with common cultural practices have, over centuries, established rules or guidelines that govern how property or possessions of a dead person is distributed where that person failed to give clear instructions before dying.

The process of planning an estate revolves around property, its ownership, and the interests held in it. Therefore, a sound understanding of the concepts of property is important.

What Is Property?

The word *property*, as understood in everyday usage, refers to something (or object)—such as a camera, pen, or handbag—owned by a person and the relationship the owner has with that object. In estate planning, however, the concept of property has a more complex definition with considerable influence from property law.

Factors affecting this complexity include the nature of the property being dealt with, the relationship between a person and property, the relationship between a number of people in relation to the property, and how such property is regarded within the prevailing political system.

Essentially, property in estate planning refers to *anything* that could be owned and the *rights* of people in or over such things or objects. It includes things like wristwatches, jewelry, paintings, bank accounts, cars, houses, suits, insurance policies, tableware, farmland, poultry, a library of books, tax refunds, pension deductions, shares, and even forgiven debts!

Kinds of Property

Property is classified into two basic kinds, namely:

a. Real Property

Real property is generally defined as land and things permanently attached to, as well as improvements made on, the land. Permanent improvements and attachments to land considered to be real property include residential buildings, manufacturing plants, hotels, garages. Minerals such as gas, oil, precious stones, and other substances found beneath the land are also taken to be permanent attachments.

b. Personal Property

Personal property is any property that is not permanently fixed or attached to land and is, by that, movable. There are two types of personal property:

i. Tangible Personal Property

Tangible personal property refers to any movable property that could be felt or touched such as computers, furniture, tools, machinery, jewelry, equipment, household goods.

ii. Intangible Personal Property

Intangible personal property is property that has no physical existence and so cannot be touched or felt. The value of this type of property comes from the legal rights derived from it by its owner. Shares, bonds, insurance policies, bank notes, trade secrets, patents, copyrights, professional reputation, goodwill, and trademarks are examples of intangible personal property.

Rights and Interests in Property

Property rights are rights a person exercises over things or objects and which are enforceable against all other persons. An owner of property has the right, depending on the nature of that property, to consume, sell, rent, mortgage, transfer, exchange, or destroy it or even to exclude others from doing these things that he alone is able to.

Technically, a person having *an interest* in a property has *a right* to the advantages that come from that specific property. Various interests in property exist, and they include the following:

1. Legal interest—this is the right to manage and transfer but *not* enjoy or use property.

2. Beneficial interest—this is an equitable right to use and enjoy property such as a trust property.

3. Present interest—this is a subclass of beneficial interest because the owner of a present interest can use or enjoy it immediately.

4. Future interest—this is a future interest that cannot be enjoyed immediately by its owner.

5. Interests limited in time—an interest in a property could be limited in time, as in the following situations:

    - A life estate when the holder of such interest is allowed to use or enjoy property only during the duration of a specified person's lifetime.

    - A term interest during which the holder of the interest is able to use or enjoy property for a fixed period of time (e.g., a person entitled to a trust income for only ten years).

6. Vested and contingent interests—a person's interest in property could be vested or contingent. Vested interests are certain to occur and do not depend on future events (such as survival of a life-threatening situation) to become a reality. On the other hand, contingent interests depend on the happening of future events to come to fruition.

The following examples illustrate the concept of right and interest in a property:

Example I

An interest may be held solely by one person.

Unongo, a student, "owns" a textbook in Architecture, his course of study. Owning the book gives him the exclusive right to read it, shelve it, sell it, or give it away.

Example II

A person may also have less than a full interest in a property.

Adio holds a nontransferable Nigerian Football League ticket to Neros international stadium, Nanka, for a specific seat. He has the right to sit in that seat stated on his ticket for each home game during the specified year—but only for that year and not for that seat forever.

Example III

An interest may be held concurrently by several person (such as with tenants in common or joint tenants) or split between several persons (as in a trust).

Bolade's father had three wives and eleven children. At his death, his will was read, and it was found that he had given his four- level building made up of twelve flats to his eleven children to be held by them as tenants in common, according to their seniority in age. By that, his eleven children became joint owners of the property and would share proceeds from it jointly.

Forms of Property Ownership

Concepts Relating to Ownership

Ownership refers to the right to use, possess, enjoy, and dispose of property to the exclusion of others. It may be an absolute or qualified ownership. *Title* is the right to ownership. In other words, to have the right to exercise the rights of ownership, a person must have title to the property in question. A *right of ownership* over a property creates a relationship between the property and other persons, assuring the owner the right to dispose of the property as the owner sees fit.

Property is owned in a variety of ways described below:

1. Sole ownership
2. Joint tenancy with right of survivorship
3. Tenancy by the entirety
4. Tenancy in common
5. Community property

Sole Ownership

Sole ownership describes a situation where an individual has total rights over a property—called fee simple in legal terms. The characteristics of such ownership include the following:

- Ownership is absolute in one individual.

- Lifetime control is absolute; the consent of anyone else is not required to use, encumber, or sell such property.
- All income legally belongs to the owner.
- Control of the property at the owner's death is also absolute since the ownership is not shared with anyone else; distribution of the property after death is only possible either through a will or by intestate statute provision (requiring probate).

Joint Tenancy with Right of Survivorship

This type of ownership has the following features:

- Ownership is shared equally by two or more individuals; it is not limited to spousal owners.
- Lifetime control is shared; consent of all tenants is not required to encumber, sell, or terminate ownership of such property.
- Each owner must have an equal share of income regardless of the amount actually taken.
- There is control at death; a right of survivorship is a key feature.

  On the death of a joint tenant, the dead person's property interest transfers to the surviving joint tenant(s). Any will provision dealing with how this type of property is to be distributed is irrelevant.

Tenancy by the Entirety

- Ownership is shared equally and is limited to spouses.
- Lifetime control is shared between spouses; the consent of both spouses is required to encumber, sell, gift, or terminate ownership of such property.
- Income received is dealt the same way as joint tenancy with right of survivorship (JTWROS).

Tenancy in Common

Here, the features include the following:

- Ownership is shared with each person owing an undivided fractional interest (as specified in the title document) that may be unequal.
- Lifetime control is unlimited; consent of other tenants is not required to encumber, sell, or make gift of a tenant's property interest.
- Income rights are based on a tenant's respective fractional interest in the property.
- Control of property at death is unlimited (same as sole ownership).

Community Property

- Ownership is only between spouses; each spouse has a separate, vested one-half interest in property.
- Lifetime control is limited (same as tenancy by the entirety).
- Income rights are the same as under tenancy by the entirety.
- Control of the one-half interest is unlimited at death (as in sole ownership) unless property has a right of survivorship feature. In such a case, property will pass outside of the probate (as in tenancy by the entirety).

Transfer of Property

There are two major ways of transferring property—a way of acquiring interest in property—when planning an estate during a lifetime and at death.

1. Lifetime Transfer

   The most common way of transferring property is by a consensual transaction with the previous owner during the lifetime of the owner, for example, through a *sale*, involving a buyer and a seller or *a gift* by one person called a donor to another person, the donee.

2. Testamentary Transfer

   Testamentary transfers of property occur after the death of the property owner and may be done in any of the following ways:

   i. Probate Transfers

      Transfer of property using the probate process—the legal process of administering portions of a dead person's estate—happens in any of the following ways:

      a. By will provision

         Transferring property by will provisions may be regarded as consensual testate transfer as the property owner voluntarily provides in his will the distribution of his property to beneficiaries who have been mentioned in the will.

b. By trust

Property may be transferred to a person through a trust established for his or her benefit by the owner of the property.

c. Intestate transfer or inheritance

It is also possible for property to pass from one person to another independently of the consent of the property owner when the owner dies intestate.

ii. Nonprobate Transfers

Nonprobate transfers of property are possible with the use of what are called *will substitutes*. Will substitutes is the term used to describe methods that are recognized as superseding both a person's will and the intestate succession laws and statutes and, therefore, transfers a person's estate outside of probate.

Some of these will substitutes include the following:

a. State law

Property rights may pass from one person to another by the mere application of established rules of law to the particular situation without any actions by the persons involved.

b. Right of survivorship

This is a legally enforceable claim by the survivor(s) of a dead person to immediately and automatically succeed to ownership of a property interest of that dead person that had been held in joint tenancy or tenancy by the entirety.

c. Beneficiary designations

This is a clause in a document that names a person as a designated beneficiary who, by that, becomes entitled to receive proceeds at another person's death. This method of acquiring property interest is commonly found in insurance policies, pension plans, funded living trusts, bank accounts, some negotiable instruments (by payable-on-death [POD] designation), and intangible property such as stocks and bonds.

d. Gifts causa mortis

Gifts causa mortis are conditional gifts of personal property made by a donor to a donee in expectation of, and conditioned on, the donor's imminent death.

Power of Appointment

A special way by which an interest in property could be transferred is by exercising a *power of appointment.*

A power of appointment is a clause in a will, trust, or other document whereby one person (the donor of the power) confers authority on another person (the holder or donee, the receiver of the power) to dispose of the property *not legally owned* by the holder. The holder exercises the power to select the person(s) to receive property that legally belongs to the donor or a trust established by the donor.

An exercise of the power of appointment may give title to trust property to people other than those designated as beneficiaries of the trust by the donor/grantor. The power given may be special or general. It is special when the holder is prohibited from appointing himself or can do so under limited conditions while it is general if the holder can appoint himself without meeting stated conditions.

Reflections

1. What concepts or definitions do you recall easily from this chapter

2. How did you feel reading the concepts explained in this chapter

3. Which ideas or concepts seemed difficult to grasp

4. What are some of the questions that the contents of this chapter sparked in your mind

5. How will you go about classifying your property ownership having read this chapter

CHAPTER 6

Situational Planning

Learning Objectives

At the end of this chapter, you should be able to evaluate the different issues and situations that arise in estate planning such as:

- Making cash readily available when death occurs
- Business interests
- Leaving money to children
- Uncertain marital status
- Determining how much you are worth

An Important Preliminary Step

The process of gathering information to be used in the estate planning process may be seen as tedious, time-consuming, or stressful by the estate owner. However, it is a crucial step that helps anyone involved to understand the need for the facts gathered and the specific circumstances existing around that estate planning time.

Painstakingly going through this preliminary stage will enable the estate owner to appreciate one of the key challenges prevalent in the country—avoiding conflicts among family and loved ones after one's death to the extent reasonably possible.

It is important, as a first step when commencing estate planning, to recognize that planning carelessly or unwisely may lead to bitterness, strife, and lawsuits rather than the happiness that is apparently intended.

Numerous circumstances that could affect all planning effort now exist in the country and across the world with potential ones developing daily.

Changing Situations

Changing circumstances include the increasing decline of traditional families as well as the disappearing value of extended family support structure, more varied lifestyle choices existing today, quest for better living conditions, access to better health facilities across the globe with minimal border restrictions, shorter life spans in the country as a result of never-seen-before, life-threatening security situations, retirement realities, adoption of foreign cultures and idiosyncrasies, the evolution of mixed race Nigerian families, return of diaspora family members for primarily economic reasons.

These situations, where they exist, must be considered by any serious estate owner looking to using a well- articulated estate plan to achieve specific objectives.

As each person's circumstance differs, a general overview of some of the more common situations will be discussed.

Body After Death

A person who is particular about how his or her body will be treated or handled after death must consider this important enough to plan for it in the estate plan.

Providing Ready Cash

At the death of a person, there is usually immediate need for cash to settle some expenses such as funeral cost or to pay off personal loans and administrative fees. These come into play even before the matter of estate distributions. One goal of estate planning is to provide ready cash for immediate family needs to enable them pay any such expenses and outstanding debts.

Unmarried Couples

It is best for unmarried couples, when contemplating putting out an estate plan, to put any property sharing in a written agreement. Unless such couples agree in writing and share ownership of specified property, each person making up the couple owns only his or her own property.

Uncertain Marital Status

People who find themselves in situations where their marital status is unclear or fraught with potential misinterpretation should take particular steps to ameliorate the consequences that they may suffer through proper and effective use of estate-planning techniques.

Some of the situations they may be contending with include the following:

- divorce,
- legal separation,
- foreign divorce,
- common-law marriage,
- marriage under the Act (west, east, and north of Nigeria), and
- customary law / Islamic law

Children

It is crucial to consider any child or children when you are planning your estate. The age of such children whether they are minors—under eighteen years—or adults have some impact in the choice of tools you may choose to deploy when distributing your assets to them. You will also need to make informed decisions as to who will provide care for your minor child or children as their guardians or conservators after you pass on.

Dependents with Special Needs

The planning for the care of children and dependents with special needs has become a serious factor for consideration as the rate of disability and special needs have risen in our society. Public recognition of other ailments requiring special care has occurred, such as autism and down syndrome. Failure to properly plan for a dependent with special needs can have disastrous consequences for that person who needs ongoing support.

Imposing Controls over Property

For various reasons, you may want to impose controls over property you leave behind—that is, to legally prevent any beneficiary from getting unfettered ownership of the property. These types of controls require use of a *trust.*

The desire for control may be as a consequence of the following:

- divorce
- remarriage,
- desire to protect the interest of a current spouse and the children of a previous marriage,
- payment of a child's college or other schooling costs,
- establishing a special trust for someone with a disability,
- restricting a beneficiary's access to his or her inheritance.

Leaving Unequal Amounts of Property to Children

Sometimes, parents want to leave unequal amounts of property to their children but do not want to give the impression that they favor the child who is getting more. Such a desire is best taken care of through the right choice of an estate-planning technique as your circumstance warrants.

Blended Families

Divorces, second, third marriages, and preponderance of individuals now choosing not to marry at all have created a phenomenon called blended families in the country. As such developments are becoming more common, people whose circumstances revolve around such families must factor in the variety of special considerations they spring up when an estate is being planned.

Some of the issues that come include the legal obligations to support dependents such as stepchildren and even adopted offspring of spouses before the marriage, the possibility of claims by step-relatives against your estate succeeding where you deliberately did not provide for them in your will, or the desire to keep your wealth in your family in situations where an ex-wife or child remarries another after divorce.

Business Interests

If a business that you own or an interest you have in a business constitutes a part of your estate, you will need to consider the legal structure of such a business.

If you own a sole proprietorship, your personal assets will be vulnerable, and so it must be protected in your estate planning. If the business is a limited liability company, then the issue of a shareholder's agreement will need to be considered as a document that would determine the transfer of the interest. A partnership business interest, on the other hand, will need to have a partnership agreement to protect your interest, or else, it may be unsafe.

Determining Your Net Worth

One key situation to determine when planning your estate is to find out, as accurately as you can, what you own or, at least, estimate, as accurately, what you will have by the time you die. You can find this out through taking a proper and detailed inventory of your assets.

Inventory of Your Property

Preparing a thorough written inventory of your property is a good idea for a properly planned estate. It helps to

- remind you of what you own,
- determine what you owe,
- estimate the correct net value of your estate,
- note any shared ownership of property,
- make a handy list to refer to when leaving gifts to beneficiaries in a will or living trust, and
- have your assets organized in case you later consult an estate-planning lawyer.

You may decide to itemize your property in detail or simply estimate its overall worth. *You may be worth more than you think!* A significant number of people who have worked hard for years and lived a frugal life find it difficult to admit that their assets could be worth more than they thought possible. This is especially true of owners of appreciated real estate as well as successful small-business owners.

Using a Property Inventory Worksheet

Section 1: What You Own

Here, list your assets—all the property you own.

There are four kinds of information to give for each item of property:

- Column 1—a description of the item of property,
- Column 2—if ownership of that item is shared, the type of shared ownership,
- Column 3—the percentage of any shared ownership property you own,

- Column 4—the net value of each item of property (or your share of it) you own.

Column 1: Identify and Describe Your Property

- Here, identify your property with sufficient details. There will be no question as to what it includes.
- This worksheet divides your property into four groups:

Liquid Assets

This includes cash, savings, current and money market accounts, mutual fund shares, readily tradable stocks and securities, bonds, and certificates of deposit.

Other Personal Property

This includes all your property except liquid assets, business interests, and real estate. This also includes retirement accounts, cars, jewelry, suits, precious stones, art works, antiques, tools, life insurance, collectibles, etc.

- There may be some minor personal possessions you may not want to bother itemising. To capture these, you may group a number of items in one category as "all my tools," "all my machines," "all my equipment," "all my household furniture," etc.
- Some items without large monetary value may have great emotional worth to you and your family. A photo album, a treasured chair, sets of jewelry, etc.
- List these individually as you desire.

Frequent Flyer as Property

A new type of personal property that you can leave as part of your estate is your accumulated frequent flyer miles. Most reputable airlines allow you to leave them to any beneficiary you name, although a few limit your choice of beneficiary.

Business Personal Property

Business personal property includes all business interests except any real estate used in that business. Examples are the following:

- "My shares of stock in ABC Company Ltd. My business UCXY Stationery Store."
- "My partnership interest in Eze, Wale, & Etim Partnership."
- "All my rights to royalties published by Wunmi Press Ltd., Ibadan (list book titles)."

Intellectual Property

Intellectual property is a unique asset or right because it is an expression of an individual's ideas and knowledge. Although it is not just a thought itself, intellectual property is an intangible asset that is a direct result of trade or work.

Business ideas, visual art, published or unpublished literary and musical works, inventions, computer programs, and designs of clothes and architecture can all be protected by law through patents, copyrights, and trademarks. These are valuable assets that require careful consideration when planning your estate to enable you to properly transfer them to your beneficiaries as you wish on your death.

Determining the value of your intellectual property assets could prove a challenge. For instance, the value of a literary work may be based on the copyright's future earnings potential reduced to its present value. Due to the difficulty of making such valuations, it is advisable to obtain an expert in handling intellectual property to provide that service.

Column 2: Type of Shared Ownership

In this column, you will list all the shared ownership types you have over any asset. They include the following:

- joint tenancy,
- tenancy in common,
- separately owned property,
- community property,
- partnerships,
- corporate shares, and
- limited liability company.

Column 3: Percentage of Shared Property You Own

- List the percentage of each item of shared property you own.
- If you own an interest in a partnership, check your operating agreement or corporate documents to see if there are any restrictions on your rights to transfer your interest at death.

Column 4: Current Net Value of Your Ownership

In this column, estimate the net value of each item listed. Net value means your equity in your share of property. Equity is the market value of your share less your share of any debt on it.

Section II: What You Owe

- In Section II (liabilities), list any liabilities—debts—that you did not take into account in Section I.
- Add up your estimate of all your liabilities and state the total figure.

Section III: Your Net Worth

Finally, in Section III, estimate your current net worth. To get this figure, simply subtract your total liabilities listed in Section II from your total assets listed in Section I.

Case Study

Akpojumo Efemure, a highflying forty-five-year-old company executive, has approached you to help sort out his assets for purposes of determining what he is worth.

He has a 2007 model XS BMW SUV, the latest Volvo S80, six black Dolce & Gabbana suits, four formal Seville Row suits, five newly acquired jackets and shirts from Pierre Cardin and T. M. Levin, one Patek Phillipe and one Chopat wristwatch from Polo, rare expensive antique collections from Sotheby's of London and Milwaukee, USA, and three personal accounts collectively totalling about N80.45million in three first-tier Nigerian banks. As an avid art collector, he has in his collection the works of Kola Osinowo, David Dale, Ben Enwonwu, and Olusegun Adejumo.

Akpojumo also tells you that he has invested heavily in an ethical fund, a mutual fund, and in numerous stocks of quoted companies at the Nigerian Stock Exchange. He also bought some of the bond offered by the Federal Government of Nigeria. He has a life insurance policy in the sum of N20.0million. As a frequent flyer, he has accumulated more than fifty thousand miles from a major Middle Eastern airline, which is transferable to his immediate family whenever they fly with the airline.

He has a consulting partnership with three of his childhood friends: Oye Sogunle, Terseer Kange, Efosa Abhulimen, and Effiom Nse Effiom. He took a mortgage loan of N70million with which he bought and developed three sprawling properties at Lekki Phase 1as well as pockets of other small debts in the course of his daily transactions totalling about N10.56million.

Using a property inventory worksheet format, assist him to organize what he owns and what he owes.

Reflections

1. What do you remember from the chapter
2. What emotions did you experience while reading this chapter
3. What information stood out for you
4. Considering the different estate planning circumstances, which ones are you most worried about
5. What will you do to effect changes in life after reading this chapter

It matters not how a man dies, but how he lives. The act of dying is not of importance, it lasts so short a time.

—Samuel Johnson

PART III

TOOLS FOR ESTATE PLANNING

CHAPTER 7

Wills

Learning Objectives

At this end of this chapter, you would have learnt about how a will becomes relevant, what it is about, and how its validity is checked:

- Testacy and wills
- The nature of wills
- How wills are made valid
- How wills are deployed in planning estates
- Determining the validity of wills

A Free Will

One of the several ways to transfer one's property is by making a will. A will is the easiest and, arguably, the cheapest estate-planning document to prepare. Unfortunately, however, a huge percentage of Nigerians die without making a will, potentially leaving their family, loved ones, and friends nothing but acrimony, confusion, and costly legal battles.

Although a person is free to make a will so that—when such a person dies—he or she can leave assets to whomever he or she likes, the person is also free to die without having made a will. This latter choice will make it possible for the government of a state where the person resided or had properties to decide how that person's estate will be divided up.

There are several misconceptions about who needs a will. Young people, as a category, hardly think they need to prepare one; but as they get older, have families, and begin to acquire homes and properties, the importance of wills in their lives increases. Making a will is a reasonably simple process that could give the person making it some peace of mind and save his family time, money, and grief.

To determine if a will is required, people should ask themselves the following basic but crucial questions:

- *Do I care about who gets my money when I die?*
- *Do I care about who gets my property when I die?*
- *Do I care about who will take care of my minor children when I die?*

An honest response to these questions would assist you decide whether to make a will or die without one.

Without A Will

As stated in previous chapters, to die without a will is referred to as dying intestate, which means that the dead person did not have a will drafted before he died or that the person's will is not valid as it did not meet the requirements of laws of either his state or the state where his properties are located, or both.

When that happens, all that he owns—his estate—will be distributed according to the rules of estate administration governing intestacy whether or not he would have wanted the rules to apply to his estate were he still alive. This is so because he failed or neglected to make such a choice in his lifetime when he had the opportunity.

Conditions of Testacy

Where, on the other hand, a person dies leaving a valid will, he is said to die testate or in a condition of testacy. Such a person is *in control of* his own estate plan and estate distribution *even at death.*

Through the will, he is able to determine who gets what property. He can also appoint an executor of his choice to distribute the estate on his behalf after he dies. By writing a will, he is able to ensure that there is adequate financial provision for his dependents as well as specifying who should care for them when he is no longer around.

Nature of Wills

A will is the basic legal document necessary to plan for death, comprising of a written set of instructions to a person's family and loved ones as to how he wants his estate to be distributed after death. This feature is the reason why wills are said to be "ambulatory' in nature—its contents take effect only after dead has occurred.

It is a document that could help a person prevent legal battles over any property he leaves behind after death. It *generally* consists of four main sections:

i. Section 1 states how the will maker expects that his final bills will be paid,

ii. Section 2 prescribes how the cost of settling the estate and any estate taxes or inheritance taxes will be paid,

iii. Section 3 states the names of the people—called *personal representatives* or *executors*—chosen to oversee the settling of the estate and what powers they will have. If minor children will be left behind at death, the names of the persons who will be responsible for raising the children—known as *guardians* or *conservators*—will also be stated, and

iv. Section 4 provides for who will get the balance of the estate and how they will get their shares of the estate as well as when they will get them.

A will could be legally enforceable. To be so, it must be accurate, unambiguous, and comprehensive.

Apart from being a record of a person's wishes and instructions, a will could also specify one's wishes regarding funeral and burial arrangements—whether he wishes to be buried or cremated—and the location he would wish to be laid to rest.

Putting as many details as possible into a will and stating one's wishes in the most articulate manner could spare one's successors the distress of sorting out assets that have been left behind at death.

Conditions for a Valid Will

A will, to be valid in Nigeria, must conform strictly to the provisions of the laws governing the operation and administration of wills in Nigeria. These laws are as follows:

- The Wills Law of various States of the federation—some of the States in Nigeria have reenacted the received Wills Act 1837 with modifications and alterations, for instance, the Wills Law of Western Nigeria 1958 and the Wills Law of Lagos State 1994.
- The Wills Act of 1837 and The Wills (Amendment) Act of 1852—these statutes of general application are still generally applicable in the northern and eastern parts of Nigeria.
  High Court (Civil Procedure) Rules of the various States that usually specify the procedure of the Probate Courts in their respective jurisdictions.
- Case Law—comprising of decisions taken by the courts in cases dealing with wills and related matters.

All the laws applying to wills in Nigeria insist on the same requirements for a will to be validly executed. To be effective, therefore, a will must be written and executed in line with the legal requirements of any of the thirty-six states and the Federal Capital Territory of the country.

Where a state has not enacted its own Wills Law, the English law of general application, applicable in England by January 1, 1900, will apply to fill the vacuum.

Nigerian laws provide that, to be valid and legally enforceable, a will must meet the following conditions:

1. The will maker (known as a testator) must be of sound disposing mind, which means he must have testamentary capacity.

2. The testator must make the will voluntarily.

3. The will must be in writing or typed and not oral.

   Oral wills may be valid under customary law, but they are not provided for under any of the legislation on wills.

4. It must be signed at the foot or end of the document by the testator or by another person appointed by him in his presence and by his direction.

5. There must be at least two witnesses who are adults, of sound mind, and are not beneficiaries of the will.

6. The testator must sign or acknowledge the will before the witnesses sign it.

   If this order of signing is not followed strictly, the will be invalid for bad execution. Signature, as recognized by law, include any mark intended to represent the name of the testator, such as a thumb print, initials of the testator, a rubber stamp, or a cross.

7. The testator must affix his signature in the presence of two or more witnesses present at the same time or signed in the absence of witnesses but acknowledged by the testator in the presence of two or more witnesses.

8. It must be dated.

9. The witnesses must sign the will (called attestation) in the presence of the testator.

10. The witnesses must be told that it is a will they are signing.

11. The will must reflect the wishes of the testator.

Key Validity Conditions Explained

Testamentary Capacity

Testamentary capacity refers to the capacity and ability to make a valid will. It is made up of two key elements:

- Age
  The minimum age of a potential testator in Nigeria is stated by some sections of the various Wills Laws in the country to be twenty-one years. Consequently, a person below that age does not have the testamentary capacity to make a valid will. However, certain categories of people, such as serving military soldiers and mariners at sea, are exempt from this minimum age requirement.

- Sound disposing mind
  A person must have the mental capacity or sound disposing mind to make a will. This means that the testator must, at the time he is making the will, be free from any illness that afflicts the body or impairs mental health. If it is proven that the testator was not of sound mind while making the will, that will automatically becomes invalid.

Three factors used to determine whether a testator has the mental capacity to make a will are the following:

a. The testator must understand that he is distributing his estate to people that he has chosen.

b. He must understand and fully recognize the components of his entire estate as well as the method he is adopting to dispose of his estate assets.

c. He must also understand and be able to clearly identify who his chosen beneficiaries are and those he has decided in his will to exclude from succeeding his estate.

Testator's Volition

The exercise of volition means that the testator must have freely made his will without any form of influence whatsoever by any person such as to influence him in the making of the will. Persuasion is allowed in law but should not amount to pressure. If it is proven that any manner of pressure was exerted as to overpower the testator's freewill without convincing his judgment, it will be interpreted as undue influence that will invalidate the will.

Intention

In order to make a valid will, the testator must have the intention to make a will and must intend that his wishes, as clearly stated in the will, should take effect on his death. It is important that he also knows, understands, and approves of the contents of his will.

If a dispute or confusion arises as to whether the contents of the will truly represents the testator's wishes and it is proven that those contents are, in fact, the record of another person's wishes, the will is invalidated.

Beneficiaries Not Competent Witnesses

A will written in Nigeria must not be witnessed by a spouse of the testator if that spouse is expected to succeed the estate. A beneficiary to the will or that beneficiary's spouse is also not expected to be a witness to that will.

The only exception is where whatever is being provided as a gift to the beneficiary is a charge or a direction for the payment of a debt. If the testator's spouse or that beneficiary goes ahead to witness the will, the gift to either of them will fail although the will itself maintains its validity

Attestation and Subscription

"To attest" a will is to see the testator signing that will while "to subscribe" is to sign the will as proof of attestation. In this regard, a blind man, for example, can make a will but unable, in law, to witness a will because his inability to see makes him incapable of attesting to the making of a will by the testator.

Reflections

1. What words, terms, explanations, and definitions do you recall from this chapter
2. In what mood did reading this chapter leave you
3. What information did you struggle with
4. What new perspectives has the chapter given you
5. What steps would you take to implement what you have learnt

CHAPTER 8

Types of Wills

Learning Objectives

At the end of this chapter, you would have learnt all about:

- The different types of wills available for use
- The benefits of writing a will
- The roles people play to making wills effective
- How wills are revoked, amended, or revived

Available Wills for Use

There are different forms of wills recognized and used by people in different circumstances. They are briefly explained below:

Simple Will

A simple will is used by a person to distribute his wealth or property where his estate is not complicated. A will is taken to be simple when it is printed and not handwritten and comprises of different sections with relevant information such as

- the name, address, and status of the person making the will,
- the named assets and the names of their respective beneficiaries,
- the person who has been appointed an executor for the estate, and
- the named guardian for any minor children of the testator.

A simple will also provides where two witnesses to the will have their names stated and signed. It is sometimes called an "I love you" will as it is usually deployed to transfer estates to spouses.

Standard Will

A standard will could be handwritten, typed, or printed from a computer. It identifies itself in the body of the document that it is a will and lists the estate property to be transferred and the beneficiaries that will inherit specified property. In most cases, the will is dated with a declaration that invalidates any previous wills and codicils to prevent confusion over which is the "last will and testament."

Attested Will

An attested will is the most common of all the will types. It is a witnessed will, and as such, it must be signed by the owner (testator) of the will and must be signed by the exact number of required witnesses.

Nuncupative Will

A nuncupative will is an oral will—spoken and not written. In Nigeria, when a dying person who is subject to customary law speaks about how he wants his property or wealth distributed and the specific persons he chooses to benefit from his estate, that deathbed declaration is taken to be a nuncupative will.

Oral wills command less authority than written wills as there are numerous conditions that must be satisfied to make it valid. One such condition is that there must be a presence of fear of death. Such wills also apply to personal property alone thereby restricting the breadth of its use.

Holographic Will

A holographic will is a will that is handwritten by the testator. A holographic will may have been signed by the testator, but it does not have any witness or witness signature. As a result, its validity may be called into question. Nigerian laws do not recognize a holographic will as a valid will.

Statutory Will

A statutory will conforms to standard terms required by the statutory laws of a state to simplify the will-making process. Such wills are made by adhering strictly to the mandatory provisions of the laws. Standard terms are implied in the will even where such terms are not explicitly written in the document.

Video or Film Will

A video will is one in which the testator is recorded while reading his own will, explaining how his estate should be passed on as he wishes. Prominent Nigerians are increasingly utilizing this will format to ensure strict adherence to the contents of their wills.

A video will benefits the testator as it enables him to explain with expressed emotions his decisions concerning the transfer of his assets. He is also able to personalize his explanations to each beneficiary. The video as a medium could offer a compelling proof that the testator was mentally competent at the time he made his will if anyone challenges provisions of the will.

However, Nigerian laws are yet to provide specifically for a video will alone, and so it is wise to have a properly written will with the video will supplementing it instead of being a substitute. The written will is crucial as well since a video will could be damaged or its effectiveness hampered by a change in technology and so may not be durable in the long term.

Electronic Will

An electronic will is an original will created and stored exclusively in an electronic format usually on a computer.

Self-Probating Will

A self-probating will is one that conforms to all the requirements stated in the laws for a valid will, but in addition, it has been submitted to the Probate Court by the testator.

Self-Proved Will

A self-proved will is written in a solemn form with affidavits sworn to by the subscribing witnesses in order to avoid going through probate.

Notarial Will

A notarial will is a will in public form and prepared by a civil law notary public operating in a civil law jurisdiction.

Conditional or Contingent Will

A conditional or contingent will is regarded as a will only when the conditions expressly stated by the testator occur. If the conditions do not happen, a situation of intestacy immediately arises as it is taken that no will exists.

An illustration of this situation is when, for instance, a person makes a will inserting a clause stating that if she dies of breast cancer, 50 percent of her estate will be donated to breast cancer research and the rest of property to her husband. If, eventually, she did not die of breast cancer and yet failed to alter that clause in her will or neglected to write another will, her entire estate will be treated as if she died intestate.

Joint Will

A joint will is a single document containing the will of two or more people who chose to make one together. It takes effect as the separate wills of the people that made it, and so when one of them passes on, their joint will usually ensures that the estate of the deceased pass on to the other surviving co-will makers.

The joint will also determines how the estate will be distributed when the second or third person passes on. By its nature, such a will prevents the second or third person from changing what that will provides or even changing their minds on how the estate should be distributed after their death. This ensures that the wishes of the person, who passed on first, are honored.

Mutual Will

A mutual will is also referred to as a mirror will, a reciprocal, will or a husband-and-wife will. It is one of two separate but identical wills made by two or more people—usually a husband and his wife—that provides for almost similar reciprocals benefits. Its provisions cannot be amended without the consent of the other spouse or person. Based usually on an agreement, such a will provides for one spouse to succeed the other spouse's estate if one dies before the other.

If, on the other hand, the couple dies at the same time, their mutual wills provide that both estates should pass on to a named beneficiary. The will of a spouse who survives the other cannot be revoked when the other spouse dies first.

Privileged or Serviceman's Will

A privileged will is a will made by a soldier or sailor in active military service. Such a will is exempted from the formal requirements for ordinary wills.

Mystic Will

A mystic will is one that remains sealed until the death of the testator.

Pour-Over Will

A pour-over will is one with a clause stating that any assets of the testator's estate inadvertently omitted from the will must be transferred (poured-over) to a *trust*. However, those assets must pass through probate before they go into the trust.

Testamentary Trust Will

A testamentary trust will, or simply testamentary trust, is one that is created under a will but does not come into effect until after the death of the testator.

Unsolemn Will

An unsolemn will is one in which the preferred executor is not named.

A Solemn Will

A will is described as solemn when it has been signed by the testator and all the required witnesses.

The Benefits of Having a Will

The benefits of taking the time and trouble to make a will is numerous, but the most important is the peace of mind that a person gains from knowing that his estate will be distributed as he wishes.

A valid will offers the person making it the opportunity to protect the future well-being of his family and chosen beneficiaries and establishes who will benefit from his estate, anticipating a number of future scenarios and determining the destination of his estate through the choice of beneficiaries he makes.

He can determine such destination by the choice he makes when he passes certain belongings to certain individuals, for example, a painting, his personal house, a family heirloom—war medals, family photographs, jewelry. Such choices ensure that items of sentimental value and strong family ties are inherited by those he is sure will appreciate, protect, and retain them in the family.

Other advantages that should encourage an estate owner to prepare and leave behind a valid will include the fact that such a document when properly drafted:

- displaces and excludes customary law estate transfer and the traditional canons of inheritance. This means that he is able to choose who he wishes to inherit his assets rather than the decision being made by the laws of intestacy.
- displaces estate succession by statutes (Marriage Act and the rule in *Cole v. Cole*)
- appoints named executors and trustees of his choice
- appoints named guardians for children especially minors
- creates trusts
- incorporates inheritance tax planning
- transfers property generally best transferred by will
- distributes suddenly acquired property
- distributes property not transferred by a probate-avoidance device
- distributes property not owned at the time a will is being made but expected to be received later
- disinherits a child or spouse
- assists others with opportunities by passing on his possessions for their use

- simplifies the effective management of his affairs for his family and loved ones when he is gone. Dying without a will complicates the administration of an estate, which ultimately increases the cost and workload of appointed administrators involved.

Additional benefits of wills are that:

- the testator's appointed executor can start acting before probate is concluded
- it is cheaper to process application for the grant of probate than letters of administration
- the testator may utilize it to donate organs after death for the benefit of suffering people and research.

Executors and Trustees

Executors and trustees are the people named in a will by a testator and chosen to administer his estate when he dies. Only one person may be needed although the creation of a trust in the will may require that more than one executor and trustee are appointed. The law allows an executor and trustee to benefit from the property being distributed by the will.

Guardians

Guardians are appointed for children in the event of both parents dying while they are minors. Such appointed guardians would make decisions about the upbringing of a dead testator's children.

Legacies

Legacies may comprise of personal and family values, money, personal possessions, or other assets to chosen beneficiaries including charities.

Inheritance Tax Planning

An estate may be subject to inheritance tax as it usually applies indirectly through properties passed on after the death of the owner.

Revocation and Amendment of a Will

Revocation and Amendment

A testator is free to revoke or amend his will anytime before he dies. He may decide to revoke either the entire will or revoke or amend a part of it. Revocation or amendment may be done, as stated in sections of the Will Act of 1837, in any of the following four ways:

i. Revocation by destruction

   The first way to revoke a valid will is by destruction—whether burning or tearing it—by the testator or another person in the testator's presence on the latter's instruction with a clear intention to revoke.

   For the will to be taken as revoked, it must be proven that there was sufficient physical destruction and that the destruction was intentional. A will cannot be revoked by the testator or his agent by merely cancelling the will. Therefore, if a will is mistakenly torn in the course of a fight between a testator and a spouse, the document may be revived by sewing or gumming the pieces back together. However, if it was burnt, no revival is possible as the will no longer exists.

ii. Marriage

A valid will, whether made by a male or female testator (known as a testatrix), may be revoked automatically by his or her marriage if the marriage is a lawful one. If the will was made by the testator in the knowledge that a marriage will soon be contracted, then the will remains valid. A customary law marriage, however, cannot have the same impact on a valid will.

As an illustration, if a testator made a will in February 2012 and then marries on October 1, 2012, that marriage conducted in October 2012 automatically revokes the will he made in February.

iii. Later will or codicil

A valid will may be revoked by another valid will or a codicil made later than the existing will with the intention to revoke the earlier will expressly stated in that later will or codicil. This process of revocation is possible since a will is ambulatory in nature.

Due to the delicate nature of a will, it is not enough just to prove that a subsequent will has revoked an existing will; *it must be proven.* This requirement is provided for under Section 20 Wills Act 1837.

A codicil is a miniature will used to alter, amend, or otherwise vary the contents of a will or another codicil or any clauses of a will or of another codicil. All the rules and laws applicable to a will are applicable in equal force to a codicil.

iv. Written declaration of intent to revoke a will

A will can also be revoked by a testator writing a declaration of his intention to revoke his will. In order for the revocation declaration document to be effective, it must be executed as a will by adhering to all the conditions for a valid will. There must also be proven intention to revoke the will; for instance, a letter addressed to a testator's brother or a document executed as a will and addressed to a bank manager who had custody of a testator's will was proven to be a valid revocation.

Revival of a Will

Revival is a way to resuscitate a revoked will or revoked codicil in order to make the document operational again. Revival is only possible where the revoked will is still in existence. A nonexistent will cannot be revived.

A revoked will could be revived in two major ways:

i. Re-execution

A revoked will or its codicil could be revived by having the will re-executed or by making a codicil duly executed, clearly stating the testator's intention to revive the will.

ii. Codicil

A codicil could be drafted to revoke or amend an existing will or to revive a revoked will. A clear intention to revive must be stated in the codicil for revival to be effective.

A revived will becomes immediately operational once it is restored. It takes effect from the date of revival and not from the date when the original will was made.

A very critical point to bear in mind is that a testator must not make changes to his will after it has been witnessed and signed. Any addition or deletion to a will that has already been signed may render it invalid.

Case Study

Mrs. Alero Jadesimi v. Mrs. Victoria Okotie-Eboh and Two Others

The effect of subsequent statutory marriage by a testator on an earlier will made by him in peculiarly Nigerian circumstances was given extensive consideration in Mrs. Alero Jadesimi v. Mrs. Victoria Okotie-Eboh and Two Others.

The testator, Chief Festus Okotie-Eboh, married Victoria Okotie-Eboh, the first respondent, under Itsekiri customary law in 1942. The appellant, Alero Jadesinmi, and the second and third respondents were the children of the testator. In 1947, Okotie-Eboh, testator, made a will, and in 1961, he (Okotie-Eboh) and Victoria decided to enter into a statutory form of marriage although they had already been married under customary law since 1942 and had, thereafter, been living as husband and wife. Okotie-Eboh was killed in the course of the first Nigerian military coup d' etat on January 15, 1966.

Sometime in 1971, unaware that Okotie-Eboh (her father) had made a will, Alero Jadesinmi and her siblings, the respondents, applied for and were granted letters of administration of Okotie-Eboh's estate.

But then in 1974, they became aware of the existence of the will made in 1947. Jadesinmi went to court, suing for a declaration of the validity of the will and the revocation of the letters of administration granted her and her siblings.

She succeeded at the trial court, lost in the Court of Appeal, and finally succeeded at the Supreme Court.

In resisting Jadesinmi's action, her siblings, the respondents, relied on section 18 of the Wills Act 1837, which was a statute of general application, applicable as at 1947, the time the will was made. Section 18 stipulated that every will made by a man or woman was revoked by any subsequent (statutory) marriage. The argument of Jadesinmi's siblings was that the statutory marriage of 1961 between Okotie-Eboh and Victoria revoked Okotie-Eboh's will of 1947.

Unanimously rejecting this argument and upholding the validity of the will, the Supreme Court decided, among other things, that:

- *statutes of general application are to be applied to Nigeria subject to local jurisdiction and local circumstance,*
- *section 18 of the Wills Act did not contemplate the peculiarly Nigerian circumstance under which two people already married under customary law would choose to conduct another marriage under the statutory law system,*
- *section 18 of the Wills Act, which was meant to protect the interest of a new spouse by revoking any will of the other spouse made before the marriage, cannot apply to the Nigerian situation where a couple already married under customary law and decided to undergo a second marriage under the Marriage Act.*

Reflections

1. What specific words and phrases do you remember from the chapter

2. How did you feel reading this chapter

3. What, in your view, were the key points made

4. How did those key points challenge or affirm what you know already

5. How would you then do things differently

CHAPTER 9

The Probate Process

Learning Objectives

At the end of this chapter, you would have grasped the following issues:

- What the probate process entails
- The need for probate and its various stages
- How an executor or administrator is appointed
- The benefits of probate avoidance

Wills and Probate

Probate is the legal process of administering and distributing the assets of a dead person's estate. It is an ancient process whose origin dates back to the feudal period in Europe and which is used to ensure that an estate is distributed orderly and properly, according to the wishes of the dead estate owner. Probate is mandatory whether the person involved died testate or intestate.

Through probate, which is a court-supervised process, a decision is made as to how the estate established in a will should be distributed to beneficiaries. The court will look at a dead testator's valid will to locate all assets he owned in his individual capacity, determine the value of those assets, and decide how to distribute them by following the provisions of the will unless that will is successfully contested by the testator's heirs.

The primary purpose of probate is to identify and pay the testator's outstanding bills, and then distribute assets as provided by law and his will. The process involves much expense, delays, and drawbacks, and could drag from between six months to more than five years.

The Probate Process

The process is structured to include the following matters:

- appointing an executor for the estate if no one has been named in the will or validating an already-named named executor,
- validating the will,
- allowing for possible challenges to the will by potential heirs and other stakeholders,
- supervising the distribution of the estate assets to identified beneficiaries,
- filing a report with the probate court, and
- closing the estate.

The Need for Probate

The probate process begins only when it is initiated by someone usually the executor appointed in the dead testator's will or a close member of his family. The executor files all the relevant documents with the probate court in the state where the testator died.

The estate of a dead person needs to pass through probate where:

- the estate assets are owned in the personal name of the dead person,
- the estate has outstanding bills and debts to pay to third parties,
- there is a dispute among family or heirs about how the estate property should be distributed,
- the testator died and left a minor child or children with no surviving natural parent.

Property Owned in Personal Name

Probate is needed where the property making up a dead testator's estate was owned in his name. This is because on the death of the dead testator owner, someone else is required to sign, on his behalf, to enable titles to those assets to get transferred from the testator's name to the new beneficiaries.

If there is a will, the named executor is the only person recognized in law to sign on the testator's behalf. If no will was made, the probate court will exercise its power to appoint an administrator. Some of the asset classes that fall into the probate process are real estate, stocks, bonds, cars, boats, checking account, savings account, or some other financial account in the testator's personal name.

Outstanding Bills and Debts

The need for probate arises when an estate has to pay the bills and debts of the late testator. Creditors, such as banks owed money, are entitled to notify the probate court of outstanding bills and debts. If they are not paid what is due to them, they may exercise their right to open proceedings for claims at the probate court.

The probate court sets out a period—determined by each State law or by the respective probate courts—within which all creditor claims for settlement of bills and debts are done. If they do not file a claim during the period allowed, the right to have the bills and debt settled by the estate will lapse.

When probate is opened, an announcement in a well-circulating newspaper, preferably nationally, is required to let creditors know that the time for filing a claim against an estate has started. If loved ones have already opened a probate proceeding, the unpaid creditors will file a claim seeking an order to be paid. If all the dead testator's bills and debts were paid up before his death, there will be no creditors to drive the opening of a probate proceeding.

Disagreements about Distribution

The third reason an estate might be probated comes up when a testator's heirs and loved ones disagree over how to distribute his estate after his death. If the family disagrees, one or more members of that family are entitled to file a petition with the probate court to resolve the dispute.

Naming a Legal Guardian

Another important reason that will necessitate a probate proceeding is if a minor child or children survive a testator when he dies with no other natural parent alive to give care. When this happens, a probate proceeding must be initiated to enable the court name a legal guardian for the minor child or children.

If a legal guardian has already been named in the will or other relevant document, the probate court will make an order formally declaring the named person as the court-recognized legal guardian unless an objection is raised against that person. Such an objection may be raised by the relatives of the minor child or children: grandparents, foster parents, or stepparents. Indeed, a governmental agency concerned with child rights could exercise the right to object to the adoption of that named person by the court. It may then follow its objection by petitioning to be named as the minor's legal guardian instead.

Where no written instructions on the matter of a legal guardian is stated in a will, the court will hear motions from parties involved about who is best able to serve as the legal guardian. It does not matter whether the testator left a valid will or not; there will always be a probate proceeding when death occurs and a minor child is left behind with no surviving parent.

If an acrimonious dispute arises from a testator's family, objecting to his plan for distribution of his property, the probate court judge could exercise the discretion to order the estate property sold and the proceeds from the sale distributed to family members.

Probate Estate

Probate estate refers to the property that is handled and distributed by the personal representative (executor or administrator) of a dead person after the person dies. Probate estate includes the following:

- all the property owned outright in the dead person's own name,

- all interests in property held by the dead person as a tenant in common,
- all proceeds or benefits paid to the person's estate at death, and
- the dead person's share of community property.

However, the following property types are not probate estate and so are said to be "outside of probate" because they do not go through the probate process:

- property owned by the dead person in joint name with another person or persons,
- assets held in trust, as long as the estate is not named beneficiary of the trust,
- accounts that pay on death to a named beneficiary,
- pension accounts that pay on death to a named beneficiary,
- life insurance proceeds, as long as the estate is not named beneficiary,
- retirement plans, as long as the estate is not named beneficiary, and
- annuities, as long as the estate is not named beneficiary.

These properties are not subject to probate even if the dead person stated them in a will because, by law, they either pass automatically to a surviving joint tenant or the property is distributed according to the named beneficiaries in each case made by the testator in his lifetime.

How to Probate an Estate

Each state in the country has specific set of laws that govern its particular probate process, giving room for variations in applicable probate laws from one state to another. However, all the laws require the following steps to settle or probate an estate:

i. filing the will of a dead person at a local probate court;

ii. appointing a personal representative, also called an administrator, or validating the appointment of a named executor in the will of the dead person to oversee the disposition of the estate;

iii. locating, identifying, and taking inventory of the dead person's property then protecting them all;

iv. determining date of death values for all the property through account statements and appraisals;

v. locating and identifying known creditors to the dead person and then notifying them of the death;

vi. publishing a notice in a well-circulating local newspaper to notify any unknown creditors of the death;

vii. paying all the dead person's debts and final bills;

viii. distributing the remaining balance to the beneficiaries—distributing the balance of what is left of the estate after all the bills and taxes have been paid to the beneficiaries named in the dead estate owner's valid will if one was written. If no valid will exists, the remainder estate will be distributed in line with the applicable laws of intestacy;

ix. filing of papers in the court to close the estate, after which probate fees are paid.

With the prevalent emphasis on tax revenue by most state governments as well as the federal government, some states have introduced, with other states contemplating, the following additional steps to be taken during the probate process before the distribution of the balance of the estate property to beneficiaries:

- filing the dead person's final income tax return and any estate income tax returns if the estate earned income while the probate process lasted,
- determining if any estate tax liability is due for payment.

Appointing an Executor or a Personal Representative

Most wills name a specific person (or persons) as the testator's preferred executor. However, the named person is only able to function in that capacity when the person files a petition at the probate court formally applying to be appointed as an executor of such a will.

When the probate court judge receives the petition, he will review the relevant will together with the petition to determine if the will was validly executed as prescribed by law. The review carried out also enables him to determine if the petitioner seeking appointment as an executor meets set criteria to act in that capacity.

Where the judge ascertains that the petitioner is qualified, he will make an order appointing the person as executor of the will. The appointment formally commences the probate process and gives the new executor the legal authority to execute all estate documents on behalf of the dead estate owner.

However, where a person named an executor in a will is not available or no valid will even exists, the probate court will exercise its authority to determine who meets the requirement for the role of an executor or personal representative to administer the estate of the dead. The laws of each state prescribe whom their respective probate courts should consider as executors or personal representatives when such situations arise.

Duration of the Probate Process

The time taken to probate an estate depends on how promptly the original of a will is filed at the probate court upon the death of a testator as well as the length of time taken by the relatives of the testator to collate all relevant documents and information required during the proceedings.

Also, the duration of the legal notice to claimants and creditors of the testator, length of time given to them to file their claims, and whether debt claims or contests of the will are filed in court determine how long the probate process will take. The claims or contests that could be filed usually border on:

- the validity of the will filed in court,
- the dead person's mental capacity when the will was written,
- the objection to the appointment of an executor or personal representative,
- the debts owed by the dead person,
- the disagreement on the value of the estate assets, and
- the way identified estate assets are to be distributed.

Since it is almost always the practice in this country for the testators' surviving family members to contest wills or institute legal actions against the provisions of wills, some testators now resort to making videos of themselves to be viewed by their families on their death, reading out their wills and laying down conditions that must be met by potential beneficiaries to qualify to inherit their estate.

However, if no claim is made against the estate or if nobody contests the will filed in court, the probate could be concluded in less than one year.

Benefits of Probate

These are the benefits of the probate process:

- It ensures the proper distribution of estate assets after the death of the estate owner as it was stated in the will, where the document was prepared, or according to relevant intestacy laws.
- It provides benefits if an estate is in debt or if the estate owns a failing business or is involved in a complicated financial transaction or a complex litigation.
- It is the most efficient way to protect an estate from a legal attack.
- It gives a limited time-frame to creditors to file their claims after which they are cut off.

However, there are downsides to the process; some of which are the following:

- delays in settling the estate among the beneficiaries
- costs of administering an estate may largely be based on the probate estate
- administration costs could also reduce the value and worth of the estate
- assets in the probate estate are subject to creditors' claims
- information about the probate estate is available to the public
- disgruntled heirs may contest a will and by that get access to probate assets

The benefits as well as the disadvantages of settling an estate through probate proceedings not only lead to considerable delays in the eventual distribution of estate assets to beneficiaries but also to increased costs to the estate.

However, steps could be taken by the testator in his lifetime to cut off or, at least, reduce the potential costs and delays by avoiding the probate process completely. The steps involve the use of specific estate planning devices and documents.

Reflections

1. What were the basic elements of probate discussed
2. What inspired you or made you sad in this chapter
3. What information surprised you
4. What insights on probate will you definitely go away with
5. What next steps will you take in applying your learnings to your life

CHAPTER 10

Avoiding the Probate Process

Learning Objectives

By the end of this chapter, you would be able to understand how probate could be bypassed in distributing estate assets:

- Reasons for avoiding probate
- Ways to avoid probate
- Joint ownership of property
- All about trusts

The Need for Probate Avoidance

The probate process is a compulsory administration that all estates must go through for proper distribution of the estate assets to clearly identified beneficiaries. It is structured to protect the estate of a dead testator on his death and to ensure its assets are distributed in accordance with the testator's instructions.

However, despite its benefits, it is established that the process leaves some undesirable consequences, such as huge costs and unreasonable delays, for both the estate and its beneficiaries as discussed in the previous chapter. There is also the additional concern that the records of the estate's assets, including information about who owns them, are open to anyone to gain access as public records.

The most basic reasons driving a testator to avoid the probate process include preventing information about an estate ownership being available to the public, saving his estate unnecessary cost, avoiding delays in the distribution of the estate assets, and protecting his estate from reducing in value.

The testator can achieve these objectives by utilizing, while still alive, several probate-avoiding estate-planning devices to structure the ownership of his assets. The ownership instruments and devices he adopts could also significantly reduce potential conflicts among his family members when death comes. Probate could, however, be completely avoided if no minor children survives the testator.

Planning Devices

The estate-planning devices that enable estates get succeeded or distributed outside probate are as follows:

- Joint ownership of property

- Trusts
- Contracts
- Gifts

The use of joint ownership of property and trusts will be dealt with in this chapter.

Joint Property

The simplest device deployed to avoid the probate process is ownership of property jointly with another person. There are two main options for joint ownership of property:

i. Joint tenancy

   This is technically known as joint tenancy with the right of survivorship (JTWRS). In order to become joint tenants, two or more people must take title to the property at the same time and on the same document. This is referred to as unity of time and unity of title. Probate is avoided where property is owned in such manner because, in law, title to the property passes automatically to the surviving joint tenant.

ii. Tenancy by the entirety

   Tenancy by the entirety is a type of shared ownership of property recognized in most states available only to married couples. It has similar characteristics to a joint tenancy because a husband and wife who own property as tenants by the entirety each own an undivided interest in the property. Each of them has full rights to occupy and use it. When one dies, the survivor automatically gets title to the entire property without a probate court proceeding.

Trusts

A trust, properly set up, is almost an excellent device that could be used to avoid the probate process. A good grasp of the history of trusts will lend an understanding of how property held in trust achieves that.

The History

Trusts evolved from the feudal law of England with its basics remaining unchanged for centuries. Then, in England, only the king could own property, especially land. Workers were completely excluded from property ownership, but following a mounting level of discontent over their exclusion from property ownership, the king resolved to grant them right to use of land, retaining all legal title to land.

Over time, however, the king allowed his workers to pass on their right to use land to their heirs. That grant subsequently became England law: the king held legal title to all property for the benefit of the workers who held equitable title. The separation of legal title from equitable title became the foundation of trust law.

Consequently, while you are living, you are the creator of the trust and define all the rights. You can also serve as trustee of the trust, which means you hold legal title. You can also be the beneficiary of the trust while you are living. You truly enjoy all the benefits of property ownership.

This is why property that is held in trust avoids the probate process. You own the property while you are living, but you own it in your legal capacity as a trustee. When you die, whoever you named as successor trustee automatically becomes the legal owner of the property.

Trust, as an estate-planning tool, is similar to the legal and equitable titles of the English system. It is a legal creation through which estate assets are by a trustee (like the king of England) for the benefit of others known as beneficiaries (like the king's workers).

In creating a trust to avoid probate, the estate owner can define all the rights and act as a trustee, holding the legal right as well as the beneficial right. That way, he owns all the trust assets, while alive, with the other appointed trustees taking over legal ownership when the creator dies.

Structure of a Trust

A trust is a financial plan established to manage one's personal assets, and it enables one plan for the preservation, enhancement, and distribution of accumulated wealth during a lifetime and after one's death exactly as one desires.

That desire is achieved through an arrangement involving specific parties: the settlor, the trustee, and the beneficiary. The rights and duties of all the parties to a trust are established and documented in a *trust deed,* which is a legal document between the settlor and the trustee. There is a fiduciary relationship between the trustee and the beneficiaries

Although set up under a deed, which gives it a separate legal identity, a trust is very flexible and versatile in nature, making it the best device to hold and manage assets both in the settlor's lifetime and after he dies. This is so because, unlike a will, a trust offers the additional advantage of being adaptable for use during one's lifetime. However, the provisions of the settlor's will or could be utilized to establish a trust after his death.

A trust is able to own any type of property that could be owned by people—properties like cars, real estate, boats, paintings, heirlooms, shares, life insurance policies, cash, and debt.

Why Choose a Trust

Trusts get established in estate planning to achieve various goals, but the most prominent in practice, in no particular order, are as follows:

- to protect the privacy of the estate owners and ensure the confidentiality of all information concerning the ownership of the trust assets, to provide for family, loved ones, and dependents, and to ensure that one's wealth are distributed strictly in line with specified wishes and instructions;
- to ensure that the management of the settlor's wealth is thorough and devoid of probate-induced delays;
- to protect the assets from creditors, litigation, or hostile government policies and laws as well as to make sure that only selected beneficiaries actually benefit from the trust;
- to ensure efficient management and administration of assets by a trusted and reliable third party so that the settlor may conveniently dwell on other matters;
- to facilitate the proper shelter of the wealth meant for the estate owner's beneficiaries as well as to provide for those who are not able to fend for themselves;
- to solve estate-planning circumstances that are peculiar to any settlor, as there are numerous ways they could be structured to suit different scenarios.

How a Trust Works

- Estate property (land, houses, shares, money, etc.) is transferred by a person (the settlor) to another (the trustee).
- The trustee holds the estate property on behalf of others (the beneficiaries).
- The beneficiaries may sometimes include the settlor.
- Legal title to the property resides with the trustee, but the right to enjoy the property (the beneficial interest) resides with

the settlor during his lifetime—or the beneficiaries, when the settlor dies.

It is fundamental that the settlor parts with the legal ownership of the property. However, he is not prevented from influencing the administration of the trust during his lifetime. This possibility is achieved by the terms of the trust deed.

Who Does What

- The Settlor
  - sets up the trust
  - names the beneficiary
  - names the trustee
  - transfers property to the trust

- The Beneficiaries
  - receive the benefits of the trust according to its terms

- The Trust
  - makes investment decisions
  - earns income
  - pays taxes
  - distributes benefits

- The Trustees
  - control the property in the trust
  - administer the trust
  - manage the trust's investments
  - oversee payments

Two Categories of Trust

There are two predominant categories that all trusts fall into: *revocable and irrevocable trusts.* A revocable trust may be terminated or its provisions altered by the settlor in his lifetime while an irrevocable trust, once established, can neither be altered nor revoked by its settlor.

The major difference between the two categories is the level of flexibility the former gives to a settlor in his decision-making efforts regarding the trust provisions. Other distinctions in the features between are the following:

Revocable trusts

- Settlor can control the trust property and pay the taxes.
- Property can be moved easily in and out of the trust.
- They are taxed as part of settlor's estate.

Irrevocable trusts

- Settlor's control over the trust property is lost.
- The settlor cannot benefit from the trust property.
- It may be used to avoid estate taxes.

Types of Trust

There are three main types of trusts:

1. **Living (Inter Vivos) Trusts**

   Living trusts are set up while the settlor is still alive, and so the settlor can act as his or her own trustee or name someone else. When the settlor dies, the trust property is distributed directly to his or her beneficiaries.

The primary goal of this type of trust is asset management and transferring property outside of probate. There may or may not be tax advantages when utilizing this trust type.

2. **Testamentary Trusts**

Testamentary trusts are created by the provisions of the settlor's will when the latter dies. Such a trust is funded by the settlor's estate and administered by a trustee named in the will.

The primary objectives of this type of trust are to save estate taxes and to appoint someone to manage the property included in the trust.

3. **Pour-Over Trusts**

Pour-over trusts are created while the settlor is alive but funded after his or her death, so it has the combined features of the living and testamentary trusts.

The primary purpose of this type of trust is to receive one-time payouts like life insurance, pension benefits, or the residue of the settlor's estate (any property that has not been specifically transferred to someone by gift, will, or trust). There may or may not be tax advantages when using this type of trust.

Trusts for Special Purposes

Trusts are flexible and adaptable to a variety of situations to solve different issues. Some of the frequently used formats include the following:

1. Charitable remainder trust

   A charitable remainder trust is structured to eventually benefit a specific charity chosen by the settlor when he or the first beneficiary of the trust dies. When such deaths occur, the charity gets the principal assets.

2. Accumulation and maintenance trust

   This trust is usually established solely to accumulate assets for the trust or to support its beneficiaries for clearly defined time frames, for example, till the age of twenty-three for maintenance or education purposes.

3. Bypass trust

   A bypass trust is also called an exemption equivalent trust, and it is established to pay income to a surviving spouse. However, the trust itself is not part of that surviving spouse's estate as the trust goes back to the settlor's estate on the death of that spouse.

4. Discretionary trust

   A discretionary trust is structured to allow the settlor to be part of the administration and management of the trust.

5. Qualified terminal interest property (QTIP) trust

   A QTIP trust is set up to benefit a spouse but with the settlor exercising control of asset disposition after the spouse's death. The spouse derives income from the trust but cannot use the trust itself or change the beneficiaries already stated by the settlor.

6. Fixed-Interest Trusts

   Fixed-interest trusts are set up to provide fixed income—generated from the assets of the trusts—to its beneficiaries.

7. Blind Trust

   A blind trust is usually deployed by political or public personalities to protect themselves against possible accusations of conflicts of interest. Creating a blind trust means that such a public figure no longer has information about or influence over the decisions of the trustees.

8. Secret Trust

   A secret trust is a device used by a settlor to provide for beneficiaries he prefers to keep out of the public knowledge, such as children born out of wedlock or a concubine.

9. Offshore Trust

   This trust is structure to administer the settlor's offshore investments.

A Reading on Trust

The Estate of Frederick Rotimi Alade (FRA) Williams

"FRA: Inaccuracies, Myths, and Secrets"

The furore swirling around the memory and estate of the late legal luminary, Chief Frederick Rotimi Alade Williams, has been the occasion for an unwelcome intrusion, yet again, into the private lives of public men. We may be excused our voyeuristic indulgence by reason of much of the fare on offer having emanated from the family itself.

That it has grabbed the public imagination should come as no surprise. For six decades, FRA towered so completely over the legal profession that a legal disputation in his household was always going to be newsworthy. The many eulogies that attended his passing speak eloquently of the pride of place he will forever hold in Nigerian legal folklore. For that reason, we must be wary less the inaccuracies of today become the myths of tomorrow.

Sadly, the current tussle of wills (excuse the pun) provides ample opportunity for the scribbling classes to look askance at a legacy that continues to unfold. FRA spoke of the practice of law as an unfinishable business; so, to seek to give an account of his legacies at this juncture is premature, prejudicial and presumptuous. Those minded to peer through the smoke and mirrors will evince from his ordering of his affairs an extraordinary mind thinking laterally and perhaps more importantly, a practical legacy for the armoury of the thinking practitioner.

Those who knew him well and those privileged to work with him readily testify that amongst his contemporaries, his sense of humour was second to none; and do not speak of his legal peers alone. For that reason, one cannot but imagine him chuckling to himself, particularly at the uninformed commentary that has attended the current consideration of the disposition of his affairs.

First, let us attempt to clear the cobwebs of terminological in close exactitude that threaten to transform the transparent to the opaque. Few would argue with a characterization of FRA as intelligent, organized, level headed and rational. Thankfully, many still at the bar, and on the bench witnessed his acuity of mind through to the end. Though in his last full year of practice, an aging body denied the country and courts his erudition and his wit, he continued to work at a prodigious rate through till the end; dying in harness, as he had always wished. For these and many other reasons, the presumption of an orderly arrangement of his affairs after his death must lie with the Chief.

Evidently, during his lifetime, his relationship with his eldest son, Chief Ladi Williams SAN was trying and turbulent. Were that not the case, he would not have so comprehensively denied him a meaningful stake in any part of his estate; to wit, Chief Rotimi Williams' Chambers and United Investments Limited. He was often heard to remark that he knew his sons well (he had no daughters), so one can reasonably infer that that knowing was the imperative behind his deliberate and unceremonious disavowal of conventional rights of primogeniture.

In 1998, shortly after the death of his beloved wife of over fifty years, Chief Mrs Beatrice Oladunni Williams, Chief FRA Williams set up a trust. As one would expect of a man with a methodical mind, the first thing the trust document did was clear the decks of all previous testamentary dispositions. By way of the trust instrument, he transferred all his assets to himself and his two youngest sons (Folarin and Tokunbo). He retained a beneficial interest for himself in the trust for life, and thereafter in equal shares for the two youngest sons. One of the trusts was subject to a specific and limited charge in favour of his third son, Kayode.

This way, FRA established the pattern of his succession, the evolution of which he supervised and put into operation in his lifetime for almost eight years.

"A trust is an equitable obligation binding a person (who is called a trustee) to deal with property over which he has control (which is called the trust property), for the benefit of persons (who are called beneficiaries or cestuis que trust), of whom he may himself be one." (Underhill and hayton – Law of Trusts and Trustees).

The creator of the trust is called the settlor. A settlor may make his trust come into effect during his lifetime (an inter vivos trust) or only upon his death by leaving the property to the trustee in his will (a testamentary trust). The settlor and trustee may be the same person; the settlor may also be the beneficiary.

The learned gentleman would appear to have carefully set up a holding company, United Investments Limited, for most of his assets. From 2003, with the knowledge and express acquiescence of all his four children (as shareholders that signed off amendments to the Memorandum and Articles of Association of the Company), he held most of the shares in this company with his two younger sons as co-trustees and beneficiaries. No one was heard to cry foul.

While wills remain the preferred route for ruling from the grave, an inter vivos trust allows the settlor to observe his intentions in play during his lifetime; and, should he or she so choose, to review and revise the terms of the said trust. In deciding not make a testamentary disposition, FRA must have been mindful of his avowed knowledge of his sons and what they were capable of. He was living witness to the frustration of the intent of many a testator by disenchanted would-be beneficiaries and sought to avoid such a scenario.

Another concern that must have weighed heavily with him was a desire for discretion. Chief Williams was always an intensely private man, preferring to live his private life out of the limelight that his professional life cast him in. He knew well that a will once filed at the Probate Registry becomes a very public document. By creating a trust, he sought to organize his affairs with as little publicity as possible. By its very nature, a trust document is a private document that the trustees and the beneficiaries alone need be aware of.

The eldest son will undoubtedly find it nigh impossible to overturn the anticipatory mind of a father so well prepared for him; he has however been able to thwart his father's desire for discretion. The torrent of vitriol that has been unleashed has cast an unwarranted shadow on a life of exemplary commitment to the practice of law and the rule of law. In so doing, he may yet find himself the victim of friendly fire.

In seeking to affirm particular assertions, depths of malevolence have been plumbed that do no one any credit. He who rides on the back of a tiger must be careful not to end up in its stomach. From the authenticity of public records to the veracity of private ones, all manner of red herrings litter the road to understanding. Even the puerile has been delivered with scant regard for good form.

A particularly tasteless disservice that Chief Ladi Williams did himself and his late father's memory was to state in interviews granted the press, persons his late father did work free of charge for. His comments were delivered oblivious of the ethics of the profession. From one so eager to let anyone willing to listen know of his membership of the inner bar (i.e. a Senior Advocate of Nigeria), one had a right to expect at least a nodding acquaintance with the ethics of the profession.

Whether Chief Williams handled certain briefs free of charge or not was a matter between Chief Williams and his client; falling firmly within the realm of client privilege. It was and remains a matter of client privilege, which the client alone can wave as he sees fit. One can only wonder at the chutzpah of a man who speaks with such reckless abandon reporting his own brothers to the Nigerian Bar Association for alleged misconduct.

Ladi is understandably upset and angry that his father chose to prick his ego so unceremoniously; but he had ample opportunity to confront him while he was alive. Even if he now claims not to have known when the trust instruments were created (not being a trustee or a beneficiary there was no obligation to inform him), he most certainly was privy to his father's amendments to the governing provenance of United Investments Limited. In particular, the amendments effected in 2003 signalled in no uncertain terms the esteem in which his father held him. He chose not to confront him during his lifetime. Instead, he bided his time, choosing instead to launch an avalanche of actions against his two siblings after their father had passed away.

Culled from *This Day* newspaper Volume 12, No. 4584 of Friday, November 9, 2007. by Remi Isaac.

Reflections

1. What words or phrases do you recall from this chapter

2. What emotions did you experience while reading through this chapter

3. What are some of the issues raised in your mind concerning the history and nature of trusts

4. What aspect of joint ownership of property in the chapter comes close to the situation in your life

5. What would you do differently in your estate planning having learnt about trusts and joint ownership of property

CHAPTER 11

Additional Probate-Avoiding Devices

Learning Objectives

After reading this chapter, you would understand how to use some other planning tools to avoid the probate processes, such as the following:

- Different types of contracts—business buyout agreements, marital agreements, beneficiary designations, life insurances, etc.
- Lifetime gifts
- Power of attorney

Other Legal Devices

In addition to joint ownership of property and trusts, other legal methods have evolved to enable estate planners completely avoid the terrible waste of time by the probate process. These methods fall into these categories:

- Contracts
- Gifts while living

Contracts

A contract is a mutual agreement between two or more competent parties concerning a specified subject and specified terms. It creates mutual obligations to do or not do particular things since each party provides legal consideration. Contracts are used in several situations to determine who will receive property if specified conditions occur.

Contracts with Beneficiary Designations

Some contracts accomplish estate-planning objectives by allowing one party to specify who will receive benefits from the contract. The person who derives benefit from the performance of a contract, where such a person neither makes the contractual promise nor receives the rendered contractual performance, is known as the *designated beneficiary*.

Certain types of property or are not subject to probate because they are governed by contractual agreements entered into by the owner and other parties while still alive. Such property types ultimately get distributed according to the terms of the governing contracts unaffected by any written will.

Contingent Beneficiaries

Contingent beneficiaries are named persons in life insurance policies, retirement funds, or pension fund accounts that stand second in line to primary beneficiaries to inherit such assets. In practice, most people who own these types of assets usually designate their wives or husbands as their beneficiaries in the creating documents.

To prepare for unforeseen situations such as the untimely death of their spouses, they state that the funds should be paid to their children or to a trust set up to care for them. Their children or the trusts then become contingent beneficiaries with the funds from such accounts passing to them regardless of the provisions of any existing will and so outside of the probate court.

Using Beneficiary Designations

To avoid property going through probate, a person could choose, while still living, to transfer his property to his beneficiaries, effective at death, by stating their names specifically on the following types of contracts:

- Pension funds
- Employee benefits scheme
- Life insurance policies
- Investment accounts
- Stock portfolio accounts
- Bank accounts

Pension Fund Account

Every employee is required by law to have a pension fund account domiciled and managed by a pension fund administrator (PFA) of his choice. The prescribed type in Nigeria is a defined-contribution pension fund because the employee is mandated to contribute at least 7.5 percent of his current employment income stream with the employer making an equal contribution into the account.

The pension fund account is a type of retirement plan with the total equal contributions pouring into a pool of funds that is managed by the chosen PFA for the employee's future benefit. The PFA invests the pool of funds on behalf of the employee in order to grow the eventual funds that would be paid out to the employee on retirement.

If the pension fund account owner dies before receiving the funds himself, at the legally prescribed age, the PFA will pay the funds to the beneficiary he named in his pension documents.

However, in practice, some PFAs now insist that the named beneficiary or the family of the pension fund account owner provides a court-approved probate document as proof that no fraud is being committed before they commence the payment procedure.

This practice is generating tension and controversy in some cases as named beneficiaries contend that it entirely negates the original desire or intention of the dead fund account owner in expressly stating a named beneficiary to avoid probate.

Life Insurance Policies

Designation of beneficiaries of life insurance policies is a very important part of a life insurance contract as well as an estate-planning device used in probate avoidance. A life insurance policy is a legal and binding contract that directs the distribution of proceeds to designated beneficiaries.

When a policy owner applies for life insurance, the insurance company will require the owner to state who is to receive the life insurance benefits when death occurs. The owner exercises the right to name one or more persons as the beneficiary or contingent beneficiary in the event of the death of the primary beneficiary. If more than one primary beneficiary is named in the policy, the owner may choose to state what percentage of the proceeds each person will receive. The policy owner can also specify exactly how the life insurance proceeds are to be paid to his named beneficiaries.

The policy owner's will provisions have no effect whatsoever on who will be paid the life insurance proceeds when he dies. Life insurance proceeds avoid the probate process. A will or trust will not override the beneficiary designation on a life insurance policy. The beneficiary designation, therefore, takes precedence.

Employee Benefits Scheme

Sometimes, a person derives benefits from an employer by virtue of his employment. One of the benefits that employers are required by law to offer employees is *the group life insurance.*

Group life insurance is a term insurance that an employer buys on behalf of all employees. It remains valid only for the period of their employment and for as long as the premiums are paid by the employer. The benefit of the group life insurance is that only the employee's named beneficiary will be entitled to receive the specified insured amount.

Stock Folio and Investment Accounts

An owner of stock and investment accounts can pass on such assets automatically to named beneficiaries at the time of his death without the publicity, cost, and delays of probate by setting them up as transfer-on-death (TOD) designations. Where stock accounts or securities are registered this way, the executor or administrator of the dead stock owner's estate is restrained from taking any action other than to ensure that they get transferred to such TOD beneficiaries.

A TOD designation also assures that the owner maintains complete control of his assets in his lifetime. The named beneficiaries have no access to or control over the accounts while the owner is alive.

Bank Accounts

Liquid assets held in bank accounts such as current, savings, and deposit accounts as well as deposit certificates are all transferable on the death of the owner directly to any named beneficiary, using the payable-on-designation (POD), thereby avoiding the probate process.

A POD arrangement is similar to a transfer-on-death designation although it is a vehicle deployed specifically for bank assets. POD and TOD beneficiary designations are both probate-avoidance devices and so facilitate quick distribution of the assets to whom the dead owner had in mind in his lifetime

Business Buyout Agreements

Business buyout agreements are also contracts in estate planning as they provide for the purchase of an owner's interest in a business when specified future events, such as retirements, disability, or death occur.

If the business buyout contract is between the business and its owners, it is known as a *stock redemption agreement*. If it relates to an entity, then it is called a *buy-sell agreement*. Where, however, the contract to obligates the business itself to purchase interests of the individual owners, it is known as a *cross purchase buy-sell agreement.*

Marital Agreements

Marital agreements are contracts in dealing with property rights during and after marriage. The parties may, either before or during their marriage, decide to enter into a contract that specifies each spouse's property rights if and when divorce or death occurs.

Courts generally have been known to recognize and enforce these contracts where it is proven that there has been full disclosure of assets by both parties with both parties having independent legal representation.

Periodic Review of Beneficiary Designations

Contracts that specify who should receive property at death generally takes precedence and are given priority over other estate distribution methods. This is because the beneficiary designation is a legally binding document, and so regardless of what a will or trust provides or your current relationship status, the relevant estate property will be transferred to whomsoever is named in the beneficiary designation as at the time it was last updated.

A will or trust, however, will take effect in a beneficiary designation circumstance where, for instance, the estate of the dead policyholder was specifically designated as the beneficiary of the life insurance proceeds on the policy documents. If that happens, the life insurance proceeds will be paid to the estate of the dead policyholder and distributed according to the terms of any existing will.

The same effect applies where the owner of a bank account, stock, or investment account or other financial instruments clearly mentions his estate as his preferred designated beneficiary on transfer-on-death and payable-on-death provisions.

In such circumstances, the contracts above cease to operate as probate avoiding devices as the life insurance proceeds, bank accounts, investment funds, and the stock portfolio must all be probated as components of the dead owner's estate before they are distributed.

To avoid this default situation from happening inadvertently, people need to periodically review their beneficiary designations in order to change them when it becomes appropriate, such as after a marriage, divorce, the birth of children, or other change in their personal or family situation.

Gifts While Alive (Gifts Inter Vivos)

Gifts are an important estate-planning tool, especially for people who want to ensure maximum enjoyment of their property while they are alive and then, at death, transfer it according to their wishes. Almost any property type with monetary value could be transferred as a gift—cash, company shares, bank deposits, mutual funds, life insurance policies, equipment, real estate.

If the owner making the gift maintains any right to the property, such as the ability to receive income from the property or to receive a remainder interest if the donee (the person receiving the gift) should die before the donor, the gift transfer is deemed to be incomplete.

Lifetime gifts help remove property from the estate that would go through probate as only properties owned at the time of death actually get probated. Gifting also reduces the estate's size and its value, thereby attracting lower probate fees that will lead to probate cost savings.

Reflections

1. What probate-avoiding tools were mentioned in this chapter
2. Which of the tools motivated you to take actions
3. Which estate planning tool captured your interest the most
4. Which tools were the most difficult to understand
5. Which tools would be most appropriate for a situation you or somebody you know is facing right now
6. Which tools were the most difficult to understand
7. Which tools would be most appropriate for a situation you or somebody you know is facing right now

Die when I may, I want it said of me by those who knew me best, that I always plucked a thistle and planted a flower where I thought a flower would grow.

—Abraham Lincoln

PART IV

PLANNING FOR BODY AND SOUL

CHAPTER 12

Planning for Incapacity and Elderly Life

Learning Objectives

At the end of this chapter, you should be able to understand the importance of addressing incapacity or incompetency and provide specifically for such a situation in your estate plan.

Health and Disability Planning

Handling your financial and medical affairs and personal care if you become incapacitated and are unable to make decisions yourself is a key development that should be considered and planned for before it happens.

Changes in family lifestyles have raised concerns to many people as to who will provide long-term care when they become old, ill, or unable to act for themselves and, if the family is willing to give care, whether the caregivers will care for them in the way they would desire or prefer.

Some people may need care that can only be provided in a medical facility, while others may find themselves taken against their will to homes for assisted care for life.

The Onset of Incapacity

A potential scenario people may face as they age is the prospect of no longer being able to make their own decisions and to think for themselves. As medical innovations extend the average life expectancy, people now live longer with the increasing likelihood of suffering some form of incapacity long before they pass on.

Incapacity is a process of gradual decline that the person being afflicted may or may not immediately recognize or understand. Apart from age, it could be triggered by illness, injury, accident, or abuse of medication or substance that may result in a temporary or permanent state of incompetency. Just being physically incapacitated, however—such that a person requires a walker to move about or needs to be helped in carrying luggage—does not automatically translate to incapacity.

When a person is officially declared to be incapable, it means that, legally, such a person is at the stage in life when he is physically or mentally unable to take decisions personally, manage his own affairs, or care for himself; in that state, he is unable to execute estate-planning documents.

Since no one else, at that stage of incapacity, has been properly empowered to manage the affairs of the afflicted person, the only option available is to apply to the court to intervene and appoint a *guardian* to take decisions on health and safety matters on his behalf. The court could also appoint a *conservator* to manage his financial resources.

Table 1: Indicators of Incapacity

Factors	Meaning	Questions the Planner Needs to Consider
Alertness	How awake, drowsy, or able to follow a conversation someone is.	Does the person fall asleep when you are talking with them?
Attention	The ability to concentrate for a period of time.	Does the person maintain eye contact, say relevant things, and appear to be thinking clearly?
Orientation	A person's awareness of their own identity, who other people are, where he or she is at a given moment, and what day and time it is.	Does the person know where he or she is, the year, who you are, and why he or she is seeing you?
Short-term memory	Ability to recall recent events, such as why he or she came to see you, and communicate his or her wishes.	Does the client ask the same question or tell the same story repeatedly? Does the client remember what they ate during the day?
Long-term memory	Able to remember life events, the nature and extent of his or her estate, and their loved ones.	Can the client tell you about his or her life, career, children, homes, and property?
Connected to reality	Not experiencing delusions or anxiety attacks. Not hallucinatory. Able to distinguish reasonable from unreasonable beliefs and expectations.	Does the client suffer from unreasonable fears, such as the belief a loved one is stealing from them, or make delusional statements, such as a deceased person is still alive? Is the client guarded or suspicious? Does the client make grandiose statements or make impractical requests?
Mood and affect	The client's emotions, such as happiness, sadness, depression, fear, and anger, and the visible presentation of the emotion. For example, seeing a loved one usually produces a happy response that is visible to others.	Are the client's emotions consistent with the situation or the topic being discussed? Are the emotions subdued or exaggerated? Are the decisions being made generated by fear, elation, or other moods that appear inappropriate?
Comprehension	The person "gets" what is going on, understands the nature of the decisions and actions being taken, and communicates that understanding through appropri-ate questions and observations.	Can the client explain his or her purpose coherently without significant prompting? Does the client have an explanation or rationale for his or her decisions?

(Culled from the journal of the Financial Planning Association in an article: "Defining Incapacity in the Modern Estate Plan" by Randy Gardner, J.D., LL.M., CPA, CFP®; Leslie Daff, J.D.; and Julie Welch, CPA, CFP®)

Guardianship and Conservatorship

A conservatorship and guardianship are legal appointments established through a legal proceeding by which an individual (or in some cases, an entity) is appointed as a guardian or conservator to act as decision maker for another person deemed to have lost capacity. The person who files a petition with the court requesting that a conservatorship or guardianship be established is the petitioner

The court bases its decision on clear and convincing evidence that the protected person has been unable to make crucial decisions on his own. This process of evaluating clear and convincing evidence is referred to as making a finding of incapacity. Incapacity is proven when the petitioner provides evidence to the court that the proposed incapacitated person is unable to make responsible personal decisions and is also unable to meet his needs.

The process of appointing guardians and conservators is complex and tedious and removes the personal rights of the protected person to make his own personal decisions into the hands of the court appointee. It is, consequently, only resorted to if the protected person's judgment or decision making really threatens his personal welfare.

In most situations where a person loses capacity, it affects his ability to manage both his personal and financial affairs. Petitions in court for guardianship on his behalf are consequently often brought at the same time as petitions for conservatorship to enable the court to make combined appointments for both positions.

The Difference between Conservatorship and Guardianship

Guardianship

A guardianship is a legal right given to a person who is appointed by a court to be responsible for the food, health care, housing, and other necessities of a person who has been confirmed to be fully or partially incapable of providing these necessities himself.

Conservatorship

A conservatorship is a legal right given to a person through a court proceeding to be responsible for the assets and finances of a person confirmed to be fully or partially incapable of providing these necessities himself.

Duties, Powers, and Authority of a Guardian or a Conservator

An appointed guardian or conservator has authority to make decisions about how the living standards of a protected person—his accommodation, health care, food, and social activity. Such appointee is expected, when making decisions affecting the protected person, to consider his wishes as well as his known values when making these living decisions.

The guardian or conservator is also authorized to monitor the protected person toward ensuring that he lives in the most appropriate and least restrictive environment possible with appropriate food, clothing, social opportunities, and medical care.

The duties of a guardian and a conservator are normally stated in the court order that appoints them. The law requires that in both guardianship and conservatorship, the court should grant the guardian or the conservator limited powers to exercise authority over the ward or protected person.

The authority may be used only as is necessary to provide needed care and services. It cannot be used in a manner that limits the human or legal rights of the ward or protected person or restricts his personal freedom. This requirement is to make sure that the decision of a guardian or a conservator will not be overly protective or restrictive of the incapacitated person's rights.

Types of Guardianships or Conservatorships

There are five major types of guardianships or conservatorships for proven states of incapacity—three of which are more often ordered by courts. An incapacitated person who may need a guardian for personal decisions, such as where to live, would have a guardian of the *person*. Where such an afflicted person requires a conservator for financial matters only, he would have a conservator of the *estate*. Sometimes, a guardianship may be referred to as a conservatorship of the person or by some similar name, or there may be a type of guardianship appointment that subsumes many of the tasks of the conservator.

i. Guardianship of the person

A guardian of the person is appointed for personal matters of the ward so as to make decisions in respect of the following:

- general care and needs and where to live;
- care, comfort, and maintenance (food, clothing, shelter, health care, social and recreational, training, education, habilitation, or rehabilitation);
- reasonable care of personal effects;
- necessary consent for medical or other professional care, counsel, treatment, or service;
- approval or nonapproval of contracts except for necessities (this power is only given if there is no conservator of the estate); and
- exercise of supervisory authority that limits civil rights and restricts personal freedom only to the extent necessary to provide needed care and services.

ii. Conservatorship of the estate

A conservator of the estate is appointed for financial matters, and such an appointee must:

- pay reasonable charges for the support, maintenance, and education of the protected person, from the estate of that protected person, in a manner suitable to that person's life circumstances and the value of the estate;
- pay any legal fees and lawful debts of the protected person from the latter's estate, possess and manage the estate, collect all debts and claims in favor of the person, and invest all funds not currently needed as directed by any applicable laws or policies;
- approve or withhold approval of contracts, except for necessities; and
- with the court's approval, sell, exchange, or purchase undivided interest in real estate.

iii. Guardianship of the person or conservatorship of the estate or both

A guardian of the person and conservator of the estate may reside in one person and would have all of the above powers and duties.

A guardian of the person, conservator of the estate, or both has no duty or obligation to pay for any service for the ward or protected person from his or her own funds. Instead, the conservator uses funds from the estate of the protected person or seeks out payments or services to which the protected person is entitled.

iv. Emergency guardianship of the person, emergency conservatorship of the estate, or both

Any individual or entity may petition the court to have an emergency guardian or conservator appointed. Such a request is petitioned for only when it is clearly evident that the proposed incapacitated person or his estate is in imminent harm or danger—for instance, immediately after a serious car accident—and that the guardianship or conservatorship is immediately necessary for protection.

Under such circumstances, the petition for an emergency guardianship or conservatorship could be filed in court whether or not another petition for general guardianship or conservatorship has already been filed. The court will grant to a guardian or a conservator only those emergency powers that are crucial to provide for the evidenced needs of the ward or protected person.

The power granted an emergency guardian or emergency conservator ends either when the time stated for it is reached or when the court grants the letters of a general guardianship or conservatorship.

v. Limited Guardianship

A limited guardianship restricts the power of a guardian, allowing the incapacitated individual to retain some legal rights and freedoms. A limited guardianship may be chosen by a court if the ward is still able to make some decisions on his own, for instance, a ward may be capable of living alone and can manage his own money even though he is unable to make his own medical decisions due to a mental illness.

vi. Coguardianship

Coguardianship occurs when a court appoints two or more people to share the decision making responsibility of a legal incapacitated person equally. Where such an appointment is made, the coguardians would be expected to jointly approve any decision made on behalf of the protected person in line with the terms of their appointment.

This requirement could create cumbersome delays in the administration of emergency care as well as difficulty in establishing authority for even minor decisions. To avoid this situation, it is advisable to name a single guardian with another person appointed as a successor guardian instead of coguardians.

Avoiding Guardianship or Conservatorship

Planning ahead for possible incapacity of individuals and the elderly is arguably the most neglected yet the most important aspect of advance planning in the country. Most people neglect or disregard or just are complacent on the need to plan for their possible incapacity because they believe it is acceptable to just grapple with it as an inevitable stage in life rather than actively plan to anticipate its occurrence. A few other people prefer to think that they will receive some forewarning of the onset of incapacity. Praying, fasting, all-night prayer vigils, and resort to spiritual healing practitioners are not the best devices to resort in this situation.

For emphasis, a person loses capacity when the person is not able to understand the nature and consequences of the health-care choices that are available or is unable to communicate his own wishes for care either orally, in writing, or through gestures.

Failing to plan for incapacity may lead to significant costs to the estate of the person afflicted as well as his family. In view of the uncertainty surrounding the commencement of incapacity, the importance of advance contingency planning becomes crucial

Incapacity Planning

The primary objectives of planning for incapacity include the following:

- Avoidance of the court-controlled processes for guardianship and conservatorship and the complexity, delays, and costs associated with them.

  If people fail to appoint someone in advance who will step in and act on their behalf in the event of incapacity, there will be a vacuum of control that will be filled by the method of last resort: the court proceedings.

- Putting into place some estate-planning mechanisms required for the selection of the individuals he prefers to manage his personal affairs for the person and allows him to create the legal documents necessary to empower them to act on his behalf.
- Putting safeguards in place that bind these individuals to a set of specific instructions designed to meet goals and objectives.
- Alleviating fears or worries about unwanted medical treatment being administered to you, or desired treatment being withheld.
- Relieving family members from having to make agonizing decisions about the kind of treatment you would want.

The estate-planning tools generally deployed when planning for incapacity give the planner control over two areas of his life that would otherwise have been be transferred to a guardian or a conservator: decisions about his health care and his finances (including property).

The tools most commonly utilized to give that control include the following:

- Living wills

- Special powers of attorney
    - Advance medical or health-care directives
    - Durable power of attorney for health care
    - Durable power of attorney for finances

- Letter of instruction
- List of emergency documents

Medical Decisions

When planning for health-care decision-making, three important issues must be addressed:

i. life versus death situations—whether medical treatment should be given, refused or withdrawn;
ii. medical decisions that do not involve life and death situations; and
iii. who should be authorized to take decisions in both situations.

The documents available to plan in advance for the possible occurrence of the three situations above are explained below:

a. Medical Care Planning Devices

- Life versus death situations

- **Living will**

A living will is a legal document containing instructions written by a person when still in good health, clearly spelling out the types of medical treatments, life-prolonging treatments, or life-sustaining measures he prefers if he were to be declared incapacitated, such as by terminal illness or permanent unconsciousness. Living wills are sometimes called advance directives, health-care directives, or physicians' directives.

This advance-planning document is important and should be made a component of a person's estate plan because the person's health-care providers—doctors and nurses—and the family consult the living will to know his preferred life-prolonging medical treatments, the treatments he wants done on him, and the ones he forbids if, eventually, he loses his ability to speak for himself. Such instructions, written in advance, help reduce confusion or disagreement in those circumstances.

To become effective, a certification by at least two doctors, one being the person's doctor, must be presented, expressly stating that the person suffers from a terminal illness or has become permanently unconscious. A living will is not be applicable where, for instance, a person suffers a stroke or heart attack from which he may be resuscitated without the possibility of permanent illness or unconsciousness.

- Medical decisions not involving life versus death situations
  To understand what a durable power of attorney for health care is, there is need for a narration of what a power of attorney is and how it evolved as an estate-planning document.

- **Powers of attorney**

A power of attorney is a written legal document that a person, referred to as the principal, uses to appoint another person to act as an agent on his or her behalf, thereby giving the agent authority to perform specified functions or take certain actions on behalf of the principal.

Powers of attorney are flexible documents utilized in defined situations to enable an agent handle a variety of transactions for a principal. Such powers granted may be general in nature, with full authority, or limited to special situations. A power of attorney is terminated when the principal dies or becomes incapacitated although the principal has the right to revoke the document at any time.

- **Special powers of attorney**

There are special types of powers of attorney created for certain purposes. One of these types is a durable power of attorney; it is different from the traditional type because the power granted the agent in the document continues beyond the incapacity of the principal.

Two available types of durable power of attorney are the *immediate* and *springing* versions. The immediate durable power of attorney becomes effective as soon as the document is executed by the principle while the springing durable power of attorney "springs" into effect only when a specified event happens, such as the incapacity of the principal.

- **Durable power of attorney for health care**

A durable power of attorney for health care is a legal document that gives an agent the authority to make health-care decisions for the principal when the latter becomes incapacitated. The power enables the agent handle his principal's affairs easily and inexpensively because no court proceedings are required to make it effective.

In carrying out that role, the agent is referred to as the principal's health-care agent or proxy.

- Who is authorized to take decisions

  - **Health-care agent or health-care proxy**

    The principal's choice of whom to act as his health-care agent is one of the most important decisions in his advance planning for incapacity. It is crucial that he is able to trust that his chosen agent will understand his wishes, take decisions with his best interests at heart and act accordingly.

    The health-care agent should also be mature, level-headed and comfortable with candid conversations. If there is a living will, the agent may be guided by its instructions although could elect to exercise the given authority to interpret wishes of the principal in situations that were not described in his living will.

    A health-care agent need not be a family member and maybe someone different from the person appointed to manage his financial affairs. It may also be helpful if the health-care agent resides within the same town or state as the principal.

These advance directives will only be useful if health-care providers and family members are made aware of their existence and location so they are reached in good time when needed.

Financial Decisions

A Durable Power of Attorney for Finances

A durable power of attorney is also used by a principal to plan, in advance, on who would manage his finances and property by appointing another person whom he trusts for that function. Such an appointee is also called an *attorney-in-fact or an agent.* The duties of the attorney-in-fact are financial in nature, such as authority to manage the incapacitated principal's expenses, bills, bank deposits and withdrawals, investments, and several other financial affairs.

Reflections

1. What enlightening matters on incapacity planning were highlighted

2. What specifically got you sad or happy

3. At what point did you feel most challenged

4. How much did the content of this chapter make you a different person

5. What would you do differently in getting prepared for elderly life

CHAPTER 13

Other Evolving Estate Matters

Learning Objectives

This chapter addresses just two of the emerging practices in Nigeria that relate to the choices available to an individual who is disposed to leaving a part of himself or herself behind for posterity. They are as follows:

- Donation of body and body parts
- Writing or recording of ethical wills

Body and Organ Donation

The quest for better health and enhanced health care means that there will always be a need for bodies and body parts. There are long lists of people in health institutions across the country waiting for different types of organ transplants. All medical schools in Nigeria are always in dire need of whole bodies for research and analysis as medical research is an ever-growing field; they are highly appreciative of voluntary donations made through proper channels.

Trade in human bodies and organs is illegal and is punished severely under the law, so donating them voluntarily as gifts is highly cherished. With more people gradually changing their views on organ and body donations, albeit quietly, a number of ways exist in which people can make such anatomical gifts—organs, body parts, or entire bodies—for transplant, therapy, medical research, or education.

There are many body parts from which aspiring donors may choose from to donate and help others. Options for donation include organs that are most often required for tissue transplants in our environment. They are as follows:

- kidney
- liver
- heart
- blood vessels
- tendons
- lung
- cornea
- bone and bone marrow
- tendon, ligament, connective tissue
- skin
- pancreas

Recipients of these donations receive them for a number of reasons, some of which include the severity of illness suffered, the physical characteristics of the donor and potential recipients (such as genetics and blood group), and where both the donor and recipients reside.

A person will not be eligible to donate the remainder of his body for medical research if he also desires to donate organs and body parts at the time of death. This is because only whole bodies are required for medical research and analysis. To ensure that one's intention to donate materializes, it is useful to contact the preferred university teaching hospital or special medical research centers to obtain detailed information on their donation program.

Body and Organ Donation as Part of Estate Plan

Donation of bodies and organs now occupy a place in modern-day estate planning, no matter how it is perceived. It is increasingly being added as a core component of people's estate plans. However, such donations are not effectively done when wills are utilized since wills are usually discovered and read after the death of a person, with potential for conflicts and contest arising thereafter.

Advanced medical plan devices such as a living will or a durable power of attorney for health care are better deployed to achieving such goals. Such devices enable a potential organ or body donor document with written instructions specifying what organs, tissues, or body parts that are to be donated to named institutions or individuals at his death as well as the purposes for which the donations may be used. A health-care agent or proxy appointed in the durable power of attorney should be informed of such intentions to enable him to take decisions in line with the principal's intentions after the latter dies.

Considering the inclination of surviving family members and relatives in this environment to contest the will of their dead as well as the general cultural inclination to abhor the practice of body and organ donations of the freshly dead, it is advisable to prepare a duly notarized document to lend legal authenticity to the organ donation.

The document, which must state the name of the donor and a list of the organs to be donated, must be signed by the donor and witnessed by two credible and independent witnesses before the notary public. The existence of such a notarized document should be made known to the potential donor's family.

To forestall disagreements among family members, complete disregard, or even inadvertent thwarting of an expressed or written desire to donate organs or bodies, it is important that a potential donor discusses his intentions with his close family and other confidantes after such arrangements would have been made.

Oftentimes, if the desired organ is not preserved shortly after death, the donor's intentions to donate will not be met because it will not be medically possible to preserve the organ while his family searches for the organ transplant instructions.

It is also important to note that there are no guarantees with gifts of the anatomy. A person's genuine intention to donate body or organs for transplants, therapy, research, or education does not automatically ensure its successful outcome. Bodies and their organs must be examined and be acceptable to the recipient individual or institutions for that estate-planning goal to succeed.

Ethical Will

People who bother to plan their estate are mostly concerned about how to distribute or transfer tangible assets that they have spent a lifetime acquiring to their families, friends, and dependents. Recently, however, there has been a growing desire to pass on more than just physical possessions, but a bit of oneself (such as thoughts, advice, and life lessons) to people who lived after they would have passed on. This desire is achieved with the use of a document called an ethical will.

Ethical Objectives

The essence of an ethical will is to help people clarify their ethical and spiritual values, link them to their family and cultural history, and communicate a legacy to future generations. It also clarifies identity and focuses on life purpose through addressing people's needs to belong, to be known, to be remembered, to have one's life make a difference, to bless and be blessed.

An ethical will, unlike a traditional will that enables inheritance of worldly possessions, enables its writer to pass on his special memories, collective family history, personal philosophy, thoughts, religious convictions, values, important life lessons and notable experiences, advice and admonitions, or a motto to live by to his family or loved ones. They are very effective in helping someone explain and sum up his life for his children, grandchildren, and those yet unborn.

The Origin

Ethical wills emanated from Jewish tradition with roots in early biblical times but has now gained broad popularity in recent years among men and women of every age, faith, ethnicity, tradition, economic circumstance, and educational level. In ancient traditional times, the ethical will was used to transmit ethical instructions to future generations.

The ancient ethical wills were mostly directions written by fathers to their children or of aged teachers to their disciples. The writers often wrote them calmly in old age, with careful composition in personal writing styles. The wills were almost always intended for the private reading of their children and relatives, as well as some favorite pupil who held a special place in his teacher's heart. The writers were usually free to reveal their innermost feelings and values specifically because they were not designed for publication.

Content and Form of an Ethical Will

The content of an ethical will need not meet any requirements, and so it could be written in any format and at any desired length. It may contain any expression or statement desired—such as a song, a fictional story, a poem, or any act that the writer wishes to acknowledge. What is important is that the will expresses the essence of writer's personality and heart.

An ethical will should not be used to chastise family or give people the last word in prior disagreement. It should be written to capture the voice of the writer and come across to his family or other loved ones as sincere and uniquely personal.

To ensure the durability of an ethical will across generations, it is preferable that it be written on mold- and fade-resistant and acid-free paper with only high-quality and fade-resistant ink. It may be bound like a book or documented in loose-leaf sheets.

Statements on the Sands of Time

An ethical will—also called a legacy statement—is the most effective way to pass on one's legacy, a priceless component of an estate plan. Senior citizens are especially encouraged to use it to tell their families what they have not mentioned before or offer them clarifications on matters or events that had been previously misunderstood.

Writing the will should not be put off since the certainty of mental and physical capacity cannot be guaranteed. The will helps the writer to put life in perspective while clarifying values. It is a gift to the writer's family as the act of actually composing it is a labor of love that, when read and assimilated, could have a more lasting impact on the family and future generations than all the inherited properties.

An ethical will is not an easy thing to write. In doing so, one confronts oneself. One must look inwards to see what are essential truths one has learned in a lifetime, face up to one's failure, and consider what are the things that really count. Thus, an individual learns a great deal about himself or herself when writing an ethical will.

—Reimmer & Reimer 1983

CONCLUSION

Planning for the inevitable (death) and the possible (incapacity) is not the most enjoyable of tasks. However, when properly implemented, it is possible to transfer or distribute the greatest amount of wealth possible in the least amount of time to those you have chosen to receive it.

The objectives of anyone planning his or her estate must be to accomplish the following:

- to preserve your assets and enhance their value;
- to assure the continuity of control over your assets;
- to maximize access to the assets by those given access;
- to assure their adequate management by your chosen executors;
- to protect personal and family privacy;
- to reduce or, if possible, eliminate estate succession or probate costs;
- to ensure the efficient and effective transfer of wealth to preferred beneficiaries;
- to indicate your desired health-care choices clearly in the event of incapacity or terminal loss of consciousness;
- to assist humanity with your body or organs after you pass on; and
- to leave a valuable but intangible legacy for your descendants in recorded format.

To accomplish all of the above, you must choose to plan your estate yourself in your own lifetime. You must also have capacity (a sound mind) to execute all accompanying legal documents; otherwise, the validity of the documents could be questioned by your own chosen beneficiaries and the courts.

Estate planning is evolving in the country; the peculiar three-tier legal system Nigeria operates makes it imperative that global practices must be adopted to suit its own environment and people for best results.

After your death, you will be what you were before your birth.

—Arthur Schopenhauer

APPENDIX I

This is a sample of a simple will:

LAST WILL AND TESTAMENT

I, ____,
being of full age and sound mind and memory, do make, publish, and declare this to be my Last Will And Testament, hereby revoking and annulling any and all Last Will And Testaments or Codicils at any time heretofore made by me.

ITEM I

I direct that all my just debts, secured and unsecured, be paid as soon as reasonable after my death, provided, however, I direct that my Executor may cause any debt to be carried, renewed, and refinanced for its repayment as my Executor may deem advisable taking into consideration the best interest of the beneficiaries hereunder.

ITEM II

All of the rest and residue of my property, real and personal, of every kind and description and wheresoever situate, which I may own or have the right to dispose of at the time of my death, I give, devise, and bequeath in equal shares to ____. Should the preceding person(s) die before me, then I give, devise, and bequeath

the said property to ____
as substitute beneficiary.

ITEM III

I direct that my Executor and beneficiaries abide by any written statement or list by me directing the disposition of tangible personal property not specifically disposed of by this Last Will And Testament. This directive is mandatory to the extent allowed by law.

ITEM IV

The word "Executor" means the same as "Administrator," "Executrix," or "Personal Representative" and refers to the person who is to administer my estate and carry out the terms of this Last Will And Testament. I hereby name, constitute, and appoint ___________________________________as my Executor and direct that my Executor shall serve without bond. Should my Executor be unable or unwilling to serve or continue to serve, then I hereby name, constitute, and appoint ___________________

--- Page 1 of 3

Testator:X__________________WitnessInitials:________________
as Successor or Substitute Executor. Whenever the word "Executor" is used in this Last Will And Testament, it shall be taken to include both the singular and the plural, the masculine, feminine and neuter gender thereof, and shall apply equally to the Executor named herein and to any successor or substitute. Any successor or substitute Executor shall possess all the rights, powers and duties, authority and responsibility conferred upon my Executor named herein.

ITEM V

If any beneficiary and I should die under such circumstances as would render it doubtful whether the beneficiary or I died first, then it shall be conclusively presumed for the purposes of this, my Last Will And Testament, that said beneficiary predeceased me.

EXECUTION

I, ______________________________, the Testator, sign my name to this instrument this (date)_______________, and being first duly sworn, do hereby declare to the undersigned witnesses and notary public that I sign and execute this instrument as my Last Will And Testament and that I sign it willingly, that I execute it as my free and voluntary act for the purposes therein expressed, and that I am eighteen years of age or older, of sound mind, and under no constraint or undue influence.

Testator's Signature:
X______________________________

We, the witnesses signed below, sign our names to this instrument, being first duly sworn, and do hereby declare to the undersigned notary public that the Testator signs and executes this instrument as Testator's Last Will And Testament and the Testator signs it willingly, and that each of us, in the presences and hearing of the Testator, hereby signs this Last Will And Testament as witness to the Testator's signing, and that to the best of our knowledge, the Testator is eighteen years of age or older, of sound mind, and under no constraint or undue influence.

--Page 2 of 3

Testator: X____________________ Witness Initials: ___________

Witness Signatures: Witness Address:

x____ of

____

x____ of

____

x____ of

____

SUBSCRIBED, SWORN TO AND ACKNOWLEDGED before me by the Testator, and subscribed and sworn to before me by the witnesses, this _______________, 20__________________________(SEAL)

Notary Public for

____

APPENDIX II

Examples of Ethical Wills

Connie Fuchs is a sixty-four-year old widow. Her husband was a pastor of an Evangelical Lutheran Church in an American congregation in Ohio. Family is very important to Connie, and she's thrilled with the recent birth of her third grandchild. This document is described as a *heritage will* and is synonymous with the term *ethical will.*

Ethical Will of Connie

Dear Children:

Here are a few words that tell you some of my thoughts and feelings about what I believe is important.

Hanging in my closet this minute is my 5th grade picture that my mom framed with this statement (it hung in my room during my "growing up" years): "Smile a while, and while you smile, another smiles. Soon there are miles and miles of smiles, and life's worthwhile because you smile."

My dear family: In reading my Heritage Will, I hope you will smile as you read what I've written because smiles are truly important.

Life has been such an interesting adventure, and you have been a big part of this journey. When I was a little girl, I had 10 aunts. Two months shy of my 64th birthday, I still have 7 aunts, and they are all precious to me. (And, all live within 55 miles of me since Aunt Lora moved back from Denver at age 82.) May you who come after me have that very same wonderful feeling of "family." Nothing beats it!

To you who are reading my Heritage Will: Please know how important you are to me and how much I love you. Maybe God should have arranged it so that we'd be "older" first – then younger – so we could've used all that wisdom all along the way. Why? Because with being "older," I realize how awesome, terrifically important my predecessor family was and now you, my successor, family, are! What would I do without you? I've said it before, I'll say it again, "Ich liebe dich!"

Comments about my values and beliefs: Remember to take time to play and "smell the roses" along the way. It's no secret what a game "player" Connie is – I coax and beg for somebody to grab a game or deck of cards from the game closet. We have to change our FOCUS at times and "smell the roses." Young people don't seem to relax (and I don't mean in front of the TV or computer). We didn't used to get so uptight about our kids walking so close to the edge of a trail or whatever. The comeback of course is always, "Times have changed." Of course! They'd better! BUT hasn't every generation said that? Doesn't every generation think they're different? So – lighten up – not everything is that serious.

Thoughts about education and learning: You have so many more opportunities with good education. That's why I squirreled away $11 per month per child ($44 total) with the ALC right after your births, to help make this happen. And that's why we made you get jobs to pay for your half of college. "Helps to build character," you know. (You say you have another name for it?)

Some feelings about family and other relationships: As I've grown older I continue to value family more and more. It's so important to keep in touch by calling or writing. You know, if I called home three times in the three years of my nurses' training – that was a lot. I only recall calling home once in the two years in college – to tell them I was engaged. But, I wrote tons of letters (3 cents postage). Thank God today for my 4-cents-a- minute Foncard!

So much of what I am is because of my two grandmothers and I dearly miss them. They were very special ladies. Life without my grandmothers would've been totally different! I can't begin to describe how giving, pleasant, family oriented, involved in church, and industrious, etc., they were.

While living in the tiny town of Okolona, Grandma Kenning helped run their store, then the switchboard. Wow! When I was 5, Grandma and Grandpa moved into our home in an upstairs apartment fixed up for them. A week before I started 1st grade Grandpa died of cancer, but Grandma remained there until I was confirmed 8 years later. She was a terrific baker, so ask if I didn't love having her there! During the World War II blackouts she came down to our living room, and we did lots and lots of visiting. (What else could we do?) She was a terrific housekeeper. Her one thorn-in-the-flesh was that she never learned how to drive a car. (Her sister said that was a good thing because she drove the horses too fast.) So when I was only 10, she started with, "Connie, you have to learn to drive a car so you and I can go all over the place!" She was a real extravert and this appealed to her! Then she remarried, and she and Henry moved back to little Okolona. Thank goodness Henry could drive just fine.

Grandma Wiechers had to be made of steel! She had 8 children in 13 years, all born at home with no indoor plumbing! She milked the cows, drove the tractor, got up at 5:30 a.m. to feed the chickens, and baked huge sheets of coffee cake every Saturday. If my cousins and I coaxed to stay overnight, she whipped out a feed sack and had a nightie made for us lickety-split on her trusty sewing machine. She bought me my first ice cream sundae at Red & Ted's Drugstore. It was shiny white—marshmallow! (We were waiting for the elevator to grind the grain.) For 25 years, she taught two- and three-year-olds in Sunday School. She came out to Iowa for Paul's ordination – and he was her only grandson-in-law! She was the rock that held that big family together. We number about 300 today.

I hope for my family, that you all continue to get along well in life. I wish that you would make specific plans for regular family reunions and gatherings. It's no surprise to my children that I'm a family reunion person. I'd get so excited the third Sunday in June every year when we headed to Adrian, Michigan for the Grandma Wiechers' reunion. (Wiebeck was her maiden name, and she was one of 13 children.) Know what? In this year (2002) the descendants of those Wiebecks still had a reunion! The youngest of those, Uncle Fred, died in 2001 (age 96).

My Dad was the oldest of Grandma Wiechers' 8 children, and what a great family that was. (I am the 2nd oldest of the 34 grandchildren.) I never heard a squabble or spat among those 16 (eight plus eight spouses who called themselves "the outlaws" – not in-laws). I happened to be standing next to my uncle Norm the first Thanksgiving after I graduated from high school (I was in nurses' training), and when I mentioned to him how well they all got along, he said, "Connie, that's because we're good friends as well as brothers and sisters!" That stuck with me over the years. Three of my uncles were in World War II at the same time.

The importance of humor: Humor should be a large part of every person's day. Laughter lightens the load and is really quite healthy. Current stats say, "If you laugh three times a day, you'll be able to handle life better and feel better physically, too."

About giving and receiving: Make your gratitude greater than your success. Strive to live a grateful life. You'll be healthier for it. It doesn't hurt a thing to thank your Heavenly Father every day for your countless blessings, though they'll seem more abundant some days than other.

"Do Good:" Do good things and stay away from what's bad for you and bad for others. That's advice all our parents gave us when we were real little – nothing new, huh?

Learning from your mistakes: Please be sure to learn from your mistakes. It's impossible to be successful in everything you try to do. You have to keep trying things in order to succeed. Failures can be stepping-stones to real success.

My beliefs about religion and spirituality: I hope and pray you continue the Christian faith and traditions of our family. This is much more important than any material possessions you pass on. Why? It's forever. And, it takes special effort – lots of it! "Passing it on" just doesn't happen.

My faith in God has helped me survive incredible challenges. At times I could not have made it without God's help.

Some personal reflections: Be courageous and persistent in your efforts.

Life is such a precious gift. Savor its sweetness. Realizing how precious life is comes with age. Youth just takes it for granted.

Hopes for the future: I want you to have good memories about our times together. That's why I'm so bossy (oops, "persistent") about gathering 'round the piano to sing (we're good!), cranking the homemade ice cream freezer, and playing all the wonderful games of "Fruit Basket Upset," "Button, Button, Who's Got the Button," croquet, badminton, cards and on and on. Agreed?

I hope you all are as fortunate as I was in finding a soul mate like Paul to share your life with. (That could be an entire book!)

Love: My love for my grandchildren is too great to express in words. They are my hope for the future and really keep me going. Most of my life's goals have been met, but it'll be mighty interesting to watch the grandchildren tackle their dozens of goals. Especially when I take my walks, I pray, "May my #1 priority be to nurture my grandchildren's' faith so as they go into the uncertain world, they'll take GOD with them and be ok.

To my precious family, I express my deep, steadfast love, because you have been a great part of my life.

Forgiveness: I apologize for the times I wasn't the Mom you would have liked me to be. But I have a feeling that as you yourselves go through all the parent experiences, you'll understand. Yes? No?

Please forgive others and me if I have hurt you in any way or if I have been too hard on you at times—it happens totally unknowingly sometimes. (Is too much discipline better than not enough?) We're too human to always be ideal about it.

A request: Time is precious, don't waste it or take it for granted. You already know how I do not, repeat – DO NOT, appreciate wasted time. Do the best you can with it – end of sermon!

Concluding thoughts: Finally, I am thankful for all who have been such blessings in my earthly journey. I've lived a good life. My hope is that you also have a good life. Goodbye – until we meet again in heaven.

My love will always be with you – you get to keep it and remember it forever, and hopefully gain strength from it, and pass it on.

Much love forever,
Mom

(Culled from www.celebrationsoflife.net)

The following ethical will was written by my dad when he was seventy. He died of lung cancer about one month after this was written.

Dear Barry and Sandy:

A few words to express my feelings and thoughts while time is running out on me.

Some standard values that I have basically lived by throughout my life, are that I have always believed in honesty and advocated truthfulness. I cherish the family with all my heart. I always felt that I gave of myself to everyone in the family. The satisfaction and gratification that I received in return is in the accomplishments of my children. No father could be as proud as your father is of you. Throughout your lifetime so far, you have more than exceeded my greatest expectations. You continue to move forward in a manner that makes me love you more and more. I'm proud to say "that's my son!"

Through the years, I've tried to take care of my family and give them some of the better things in life. I tried and succeeded in being able to give my children a good education. Although I was only a working man, many was the time I worked two jobs for the extra money so that the family could have a little bit more. I had often thought of going into some kind of business, but I didn't have the expertise in any particular field, or the finances to afford the luxury of risk. However, I'm proud to say that you have shown me through the years, the aggressiveness that I lacked emerged in you.

I have tried to be financially sound and leave behind an adequate amount of finances to carry your mother through the rest of her days. Being no one can predict the future, I ask that should it ever be necessary, see that your mother remains comfortable financially and otherwise.

Sandy, you have always made me proud with your accomplishments and different endeavors. You have never undertaken a task that was under-achieved. Through the years you have been in my confidence and as close as a daughter. I love you and the girls deeply.

My concentration is not too great at this point as I'm sure I can say much more. Barry could not have picked a finer mate. You are a good wife and excellent mother. I feel a father and daughter relation to you.

I hope Alisha and Hannah follow in the footsteps of the family and their traditions. I love you all.

Dad

(An excerpt from Dr. Braine's book Ethical Wills: Putting your Values on Paper)

RESOURCES

1. Abayomi, Kole. *Wills: Law and Practice.* Lagos: Mbeyi & Associates. 2004. Print.
2. Brock, Fred. *Retire on Less Than You Think: The New York Times Guide to Planning Your Financial Future.* New York: Times Books. 2004. Print.
3. Chattertom, David A. *Pensions Law and Practice.* London: Cavendish. 1998. Print.
4. Clifford, Denis, and Jordan, Cora. *Plan Your Estate.* 6th Edition. CA, U.S.A: Nolo. 2002. Print.
5. Graham, Benjamin, updated with commentary by Zweig, Jason. *The Intelligent Investor.* Revised Edition. New York. Harper Collins. 2003. Print.
6. Hallman, Victor G., Ph. D., J.D., and Rosenbloom, Jerry S., Ph.D. *Personal Financial Planning.* 7th Edition. New York: McGraw-Hill. 2003. Print.
7. Kiyosaki, Robert T., and Lechter, Sharon L., CPA. *Retire Young Retire Rich.* New York: Warner Books. 2002. Print.
8. Lochray, Paul J. *Financial Planner's Guide to Estate Planning.* 3rd Edition. New Jersey: Prentice-Hall. 1992. Print.
9. Mittra, Sid. *Practicing Financial Planning – A Complete Guide for Professionals.* Michigan: Mittra & Asociates. 1993. Print.
10. Morris, Kenneth M., and Siegel, Alan M. *The Wall Street Journal: Guide to Understanding Personal Finance.* New York: Lightbulb Press and Dow Jones & Co. 1997. Print.

11. Musalem, Alberto R., and Palacios, Robert J, ed. *Public Pension Fund Management: Governance, Accountability and Investment Policies.* Washington D.C.: The World Bank. 2004. Print.
12. Nelson, Theron R., and Potter, Thomas A. *Real Estate Law-Concepts and Applications.* Minneapolis: West. 1994. Print.
13. Odulana, Femi O., FCA, MAAA. *Pension Reforms in Nigeria: A Guide to the Implementation and Operation of the Pension Reform Act 2004.* Lagos: Chartered Institute of Bankers of Nigeria. 2007. Print.
14. Okonkwo, C.O. *Introduction to Nigerian Law.* London: Sweet & Maxwell. 1980. Print.
15. Orman, Suze. *The Road to Wealth – A Comprehensive Guide to Your Money.* New York: Riverhead. 2001. Print.
16. Petras, Kathryn & Ross. *The Only Retirement Guide You'll Ever Need.* New York: Poseidon Press. 1991. Print.
17. Prestopino, Chris J., and Bost, John C. *Estate Planning and Taxation.* 1996 Annual Edition. U.S.A. Kendall/Hunt. 1996
18. Schwab, Charles R. *You're Fifty – Now What?: Investing for the Second Half of Your Life.* New York: Three Rivers. 2001. Print.
19. Slesnick, Twila, Ph. D., Enrolled Agent, and Suttle, John C., CPA. *Creating Your Own Retirement Plan – A Guide to Keoghs & IRAs for the Self-Employed.* 2nd Edition. CA, U.S.A: Nolo. 2002. Print.
20. Teitelbaum, David F. *The Procrastinator's Guide to Financial Security.* New York: AMACOM.2001. Print.
21. Udenze, Mbanugo. *Pension Law & Practice in Nigeria: A Review of the Pension Reform Act 2004.* Lagos: Mbanugo & Udenze. 2006. Print.
22. Wolf, Harold A. *Personal Financial Planning.* 2nd Edition. Texas: Ginn Press. 1992. Print.
23. Isaac, Remi. *This Day* Newspaper. *"FRA: Inaccuracies, Myths and Secrets"* Vol. 12, No 4584 of November 9, 2007.

24. Ezeilo, Joy, LL.M., B.L. "Law and Practices Relating to Women's Inheritance Rights in Nigeria: An Overview." wacolnigeria.org. Web.
25. Gardner, Randy J.D., LL.M., CPA, CFP, Daff, Leslie, J.D., and Weld CPA, CFP. Journal of the Financial Planning Association. "Defining Capacity in the Modern Estate Plan." Web
26. Hopkins, Earl P. chestofbooks.com. "Canons of Descent" excerpts from Handbook on the Law. Web.
27. Itua, Paul Okhaide. Journal of Law & Conflict Resolution." Legitimacy, Legitimation, and Succession in Nigeria: An Appraisal of Section 42(2) of the Constitution of the Federal Republic of Nigeria 1999 as amended on the Rights of Inheritance." Vol. 4(3)pp. 31–44, March 2012. Web.
28. Layton, Deborah. .netplaces/articles. "Creating a Trust." Web.
29. Marsh, Tia. Adoption Publishing Company. "Full Protection under the Law: Wills, Guardianship, Life Insurance, Re-adoption, Citizenship." Web
30. Onuoha, Akujobi Reginald.icnl.org. "Discriminatory Property Inheritance Under Customary Law in Nigerian: NGOs to the Rescue." Web.
31. Ozoemena, Smatt. "Legal Aspects of Administration of Estate in Nigeria." Web.
32. www.apps.leg.wa.gov/RCW/. "Guardianship Basics - FAQ" Web.
33. www.fitzwatermeyer.com/articles. "Incapacity Issues." Web.
34. www.definitions.uslegal.com.
35. www.expertlaw.com/library
36. www.moneyover55.about.com

GLOSSARY

Administration. The court-supervised distribution of an estate during probate. Also used to describe the same process for a trust after the grantor dies.

Administrator. A person appointed or who petitions to administer an estate in an intestate succession. The antiquated English term of **administratrix** was used to refer to a female but is generally no longer in standard legal usage.

Advance medical directive. The legal instrument in which a person nominates another to make medical decisions when one is unable to do so and also expresses the person's wishes as to the extent of "extraordinary" medical care desired in case of imminent death from an irreversible condition or in the case of a persistent vegetative state. The advance medical directive includes both a "living will" and a "durable power of attorney for health-care decisions."

Attorney-in-fact. The person appointed under a power of attorney to conduct the affairs and deal with the property of another. The attorney-in-fact need not be a lawyer; any competent adult individual may serve. Under many recent state statutes, the term "attorney-in-fact" has been replaced by the term "agent" under the Uniform Powers of Attorney Act.

Asset. Anything a person owns that has value, such as your home and other real estate, bank accounts, life insurance, investments, furniture, jewelry, art, clothing, and collectibles

Assignment. A short document that transfers your interest in assets from your name to another. Often used when transferring assets to a trust.

Beneficiary. Anyone receiving a gift or benefitting from a trust, pension fund, insurance policy, or retirement plan to take assets under a will. The beneficiary has "equitable title" to a trust property.

Bequest. A testamentary gift of personal property traditionally other than money.

Capacity. The legal competence to effectively perform a given act (e.g. to write a will or trust or to enter into a binding contract).

Claims. A dead person's creditors may file claims against the dead person's estate to collect any outstanding debt owed by the former.

Codicil. (1) An amendment to a will; (2) a will that modifies or partially revokes an existing or

earlier will.

Conservator. One who is legally responsible for the care and well-being of another person. If appointed by a court, the conservator is under the court's supervision. May also be called a guardian.

Conservatorship. A court-controlled program for persons who are unable to manage their own affairs due to mental or physical incapacity by virtue of being a minor. May also be called a guardianship.

Contest. To dispute or challenge the terms of a will or trust.

Creditor. Person or institution to whom money is owed.

Deceased. A dead person.

Deed. A document that lets you transfer title of your real estate to another person(s).

Descent. Succession to real property.

Distribution. Payment in cash or asset(s) to one who is entitled to receive it.

Disinherit. To prevent someone from inheriting from you.

Durable power of attorney for asset management. A legal document that gives another person full or limited legal authority to sign your name on your behalf in your absence. Valid through incapacity and ends at death.

Durable power of attorney for health care. A legal document that lets you give someone else the authority to make health-care decisions for you in the event you are unable to make them.

Estate. Assets and debts left by an individual at death.

Estate taxes. Taxes on the value of assets left at death. Also called inheritance taxes or death taxes.

Estate planning. The process of arranging one's property and affairs so as to ensure their current management and ultimate disposition in the most efficient, effective, economical, and private manner, taking into consideration the effect of tax and administrative laws and regulations.

Equity. The current market value of an asset less any loan or liability.

Equitable title. Beneficial ownership of an asset; the right to use, spend, consume, and/or enjoy an asset or its income.

Executor/executrix or **personal representative** (PR). Person or institution named to administer the estate, generally subject to the supervision of the probate court, in accordance with the testator's wishes in the will. In most cases, the testator will nominate an executor/PR in the will unless that person or institution is unable or unwilling to serve. Female is executrix.

Fiduciary. Person having the legal duty to act primarily for another's benefit.

Fiduciary responsibility. A serious responsibility of trust imposed upon one by the law, requiring the utmost degree of integrity and prudence in dealing with the property entrusted to the fiduciary (e.g., trustee, administrator, executor, guardian, conservator, agent).

Funding. The process of transferring assets to your living trust.

General power of attorney. A document that gives the attorney-in-fact broad, plenary powers. Most comprehensive estate plans include a general durable power-of-attorney.

Gift. A transfer from one individual to another without fair compensation

Gift deed. Also called a deed of gift or gift conveyance. A mechanism used in giving property during the giver's lifetime to another person for little or no compensation.

Grantor. The person who sets up or creates the trust. The person whose trust it is. Also called creator, settlor, trustor, donor, or trustmaker.

Gross estate. The value of an estate before debts are paid.

Guardianship. See Conservatorship.

Health-care proxy. See **Durable power of attorney for health care**.

Heir. A person entitled to inherit all or a portion of the estate of a person who died without a will. Technically, beneficiaries are different from heirs. Heirs are people who may or actually do inherit estate assets from a dead person under the laws of intestacy. Beneficiaries take assets under will provisions.

Holographic will. A handwritten will.

Incapacitated/Incompetent. Unable to manage one's own affairs either temporarily or permanently. Lack of legal power.

Inheritance. The assets received from someone who has died.

Inheritor. A beneficiary in a succession, testate or intestate.

Inter vivos. Latin term that means "between the living." An inter vivos trust is created while you are living instead of after you die. A revocable living trust is an inter vivos trust.

Irrevocable trust. A trust that cannot be changed (revoked) or cancelled once it is set up. Opposite of revocable trust.

Intestate. A person who has not created a will or who does not have a valid will at the time of death.

Intestacy. The distribution of estate assets when a person dies without a will.

Joint Ownership. When two or more persons own the same asset.

Joint tenants with rights of survivorship. A form of joint ownership in which the deceased owner's share automatically and immediately transfers to the surviving joint tenant(s).

Jurisdiction. The power or authority of a court to hear and decide a particular matter. Jurisdiction may be limited by geographic area or by the type of case being heard.

Legal title. "Registered ownership" of an asset. Refers to the person(s) whose name is on the deed, signature card, registration certificate, etc.

Liquid assets. Cash and other assets (like stocks) that can easily be converted into cash.

Living trust. A written legal document that creates an entity to which you transfer ownership of your assets. Contains your instructions for managing your assets during your lifetime and for their distribution upon your incapacity or death. Avoids probate at death and court control of assets at incapacity. Also called a revocable inter vivos trust. A trust created during one's lifetime.

Living will. The instrument used to express one's wishes for treatment in the event of irreversible terminal condition or persistent vegetative state. Now often replaced by advance medical directive.

Net estate. The value of an estate after all debts have been paid.

Net value. The current market value of an asset less any loan or debt.

Payable-on-death. A bank account titled in the name of the original owner, but directing distribution to a named beneficiary upon the owner's death. POD accounts avoid probate administration.

Per capita. A way of distributing your estate so that your surviving descendants will share equally, regardless of their generation.

Per stirpes. A way of distributing your estate so that your surviving descendents will receive only what their immediate ancestor would have received if he/she had been living at your death.

Personal property. Movable property. Includes furniture, automobiles, equipment, cash, and stocks. Opposite of real property that is permanent (like land).

Personal representative. Another name for an executor or administrator.

Probate. A legal process of settling the estate of a deceased person.

Pour-over will. A will used in conjunction with a revocable living trust to dispose of any property owned by the deceased at time of death which was not transferred to the trust during the trustor's lifetime. The pour-over will also revokes all prior wills, but unlike traditional wills, it does not contain detailed dispositive provisions; rather it directs distribution of all individually owned property of the testator to the trustee of his/her trust. The trust instrument contains detailed instructions relating to the distribution of the property. Like all wills, a pour-over will is subject to probate administration.

Power of attorney. A legal document giving someone legal authority to sign your name on your behalf in your absence. Ends at incapacity (unless it is a *durable* power of attorney) or death.

Probate. The legal process, usually administered by a probate court or an official subject to the court's authority, established to supervise the transfer of legal title to property from a dead person to his heirs or beneficiaries or to supervise the management of the property and affairs of one incapable of handling his or her own affairs.

Probate estate. The assets that go through probate after you die. Usually this includes assets you own in your name and those paid to your estate. Usually does not include assets owned jointly, payable-on-death accounts, insurance and other assets with beneficiary designations. Assets in a trust also do not go through probate.

Probate fees. Legal, executor, and appraisal fees and court costs when an estate goes through probate. Probate fees are paid from assets in the estate before the assets are fully distributed to the heirs.

Real property. Land and property that is permanently attached to land (like a building or a house).

Revocable trust. A trust in which the person setting it up retains the power to change (revoke) or cancel the trust during his/her lifetime. Opposite of irrevocable trust.

Settle an estate. The process of handling the final affairs (valuation of assets, payment of debts and taxes, distribution of assets to beneficiaries) after someone dies.

Settlor. See Grantor.

Spouse. Husband or wife.

Surviving spouse. The spouse who is living after one spouse has died.

Successor trustee. Person or institution named in the trust document who will take over should the first trustee die, resign, or otherwise become unable to act.

Tangible personal property. Personal property that, ordinarily, has no registered ownership attached to it, e.g., furniture, clothing, jewelry, antiques, collections, etc., but not cash or other financial assets.

Tenants-in-common. A form of co-ownership in which a deceased tenant's share passes to his/her heirs or beneficiaries through his/her estate under the terms of a will or in accordance with the laws of intestate succession in the absence of a will.

Tenants-by-the-entirety. A form of co-ownership of property available *only* to married couples; very similar to joint tenancy in that title to the property automatically rests in the surviving spouse tenant-by-the-entirety.

Testamentary trust. A trust established in a person's will. A testamentary trust only comes into operation after the will has been probated and the assets have been distributed in accordance with the probate court order. In many states, testamentary trusts remain subject to the jurisdiction of the probate court.

Testate. A person who dies having created a will before death.

Testator. A person who executes or signs a will; that is, the person whose will it is. The antiquated English term of **testatrix** is used to refer to a female.

Title. Document proving ownership of an asset.

Trust. A legal arrangement in which "legal title" (registered ownership) to assets is transferred to a "trustee" who thereafter has a fiduciary duty to manage and distribute the trust assets for the benefit of the beneficiaries of the trust all in accordance with the instructions contained in the trust document ("declaration of trust"). The beneficiaries hold "equitable title" (right to use and enjoy) to those assets. Trusts of various types are frequently used in estate planning to achieve tax, financial, and personal objectives. It is helpful to remember that *every trust is simply a set of your instructions.*

Trust company. An institution that specializes in managing trusts. Also called a corporate trustee.

Trustee. One who holds *legal* title to trust assets, managing and distributing those assets in accordance with the terms and conditions specified in the declaration of trust. A trustee may be an individual or a bank or trust company licensed to serve as a trustee. A trust may have one or more trustees (cotrustees) who act together.

Trustor. See Grantor.

Trust deed. Document creating the trust.

Trust estate. Also known as trust corpus or trust property. The assets transferred to the trustee by reregistering their legal titles in the name of the trustee. The trust Estate can include real estate, bank accounts, stocks, bonds, brokerage accounts, partnership interests, tangible personal property, and many other types of financial and legal interests.

Unfunded. Your living trust is unfunded if you have not transferred assets into it.

Will. A written legal document setting out instructions for disposing of one's property after one's death. A will can only be enforced through the probate court.

INDEX

Made in United States
Orlando, FL
04 November 2026

90204428R00141